Conversations with
Isaac Bashevis Singer

Other Books by Isaac Bashevis Singer

LOVE AND EXILE
STORIES FOR CHILDREN
THE FAMILY MOSKAT
SATAN IN GORAY
THE SPINOZA OF MARKET STREET
THE MAGICIAN OF LUBLIN
THE SLAVE
SHORT FRIDAY AND OTHER STORIES
THE MANOR
THE ESTATE
THE SÉANCE
A FRIEND OF KAFKA
A CROWN OF FEATHERS
IN MY FATHER'S COURT
ENEMIES, A LOVE STORY
PASSIONS
A LITTLE BOY IN SEARCH OF GOD
A YOUNG MAN IN SEARCH OF LOVE
SHOSHA
OLD LOVE
LOST IN AMERICA
THE REACHES OF HEAVEN
THE COLLECTED STORIES OF ISAAC
  BASHEVIS SINGER
THE PENITENT
YENTL THE YESHIVA BOY

Other Books by Richard Burgin

CONVERSATIONS WITH JORGE LUIS
  BORGES
THE MAN WITH MISSING PARTS, *with J. M.
  Alonso*

Conversations with Isaac Bashevis Singer

*Isaac Bashevis Singer
and Richard Burgin*

Doubleday & Company, Inc.
Garden City, New York
1985

Portions of this book appeared in *The New York
Times Magazine* (in two parts). Other selections
appeared in *Vogue, Michigan Quarterly Review,
Chicago Review, The Hudson Review,* and
Saturday Review. The authors are grateful to the
editors of all these publications.

Library of Congress Cataloging in Publication Data

Singer, Isaac Bashevis, 1904–
    Conversations with Isaac Bashevis Singer.

    1. Singer, Isaac Bashevis, 1904–
—Interviews.
I. Burgin, Richard.   II. Title.
PJ5129.S49Z462   1985   839'.0933 [B]
ISBN 0-385-17999-5
Library of Congress Catalog Card Number 85-1490

Printed in the United States of America

Designed by Judith Neuman

First Edition

Contents

viii

Introductory Note

I met Isaac Bashevis Singer in September 1976 in New York. After our first meeting I decided to read everything he'd published in English, and shortly thereafter received permission to interview him about his life and work. Most of my interviews were conducted in Mr. Singer's New York apartment; the rest took place in his condominium in Surfside, Florida. All of our conversations were tape-recorded and subsequently revised by Mr. Singer and myself.

After Singer won the Nobel Prize for Literature in 1978, the progress of this book was somewhat interrupted. He was inundated by various literary, theatrical, and film projects, as well as by a good deal of the world's media. In retrospect, I consider this hiatus a blessing for this book, for it allowed me the time to mature both as a reader and as a human being. When I interviewed him for the last time, in March 1983, I had a stronger grasp of Singer's work and character than I had in 1976.

It is the character of Isaac Bashevis Singer and the way it perceives and fashions the world that is the subject of this book. Although Singer believes that a writer should be careful not to submit someone to too much analysis, I want to mention one quality of his that's important for the reader of these pages to remember. Singer is a remarkably honest man, but because he thinks, lives in, and creates a world of deep and vivid contradictions, it is not a "simple" honesty. As with

x

Robert Frost, it's easy not only to misread Singer but to misperceive him as a human personality as well. In talking to him, as in reading him, one must learn to adjust to a mind that not only is original but insists, however unfashionable it might be, on telling you exactly what it thinks. This, of course, is one of the qualities that make him precious to his readers and to people like myself who have been given the chance to know him.

Richard Burgin

1.

Look into the human ocean . . . Distortion and logic . . . The Rabbi's life . . . A well which is never exhausted . . . A childhood dream

SINGER: Every life is strange. In my case, for some reason, I attract strange people. The people who come to see me and who are interested in me are often strange and their stories are often terribly crazy and at the same time true.

BURGIN: What gives them the courage to tell you stories about their lives?

SINGER: Because I ask them, not in a professional way, but in a natural way: How do you live? Are you married, and if you are not married, do you have a boyfriend or a girlfriend? I get them to tell stories. As a matter of fact, when they ask me about my private life, I tell them. I'm also eager to tell. Let's say I would meet a half-*meshuga* person who tells me all kinds of things and then if he says, "How about you?" I won't say, "It's none of your business." I feel that just as I want to hear about him, he's entitled to hear about me and I will tell him many of the strange things in my life. This visitor with his secret is, after all, part of the big universe. If he tells me that he has divorced fifteen wives, I'd like to hear what he has to say. I'm sure that in the process of his telling it, I will hear something which is completely new as far as my knowledge of human beings is concerned. I may use him in my writing.

Literature is not enriched by a man who is all the time looking into himself, but by a writer who looks into other people. The more you see what other people do, the more you learn about yourself. The experiments which the modernists make all deal with form, with what they call form, with silly things—whether to punctuate a poem or not to punctuate, whether to sign with capital letters or with small letters. This is of no value. I say to myself, why don't they look into the human ocean which surrounds them where stories and novelties flow by the millions? It's there where my experiments take place—in the laboratory of humanity, not on a piece of paper.

BURGIN: I wonder if you still make use of your laboratory of childhood memories. If not, I'm still interested in what your earliest or most powerful recollections are from childhood.

SINGER: Art generally, and literature specifically, are connected with memory. The real writers have all had good memories, they remember their childhood, while many people don't. If you read Tolstoy's *Childhood* you must come to admire his great memory. I don't compare myself to this master, but my memory is very good. I remember things that happened when I was three years old and I even have proof that I remember things which happened when I was two and a half years old, because we lived in a little village called Leonczyn and we moved out when I was less than three years old. I once spoke to my mother and described this place and the names of the people and she could not believe it. I still see all this as if it happened yesterday. Of course, when I worked on *In My Father's Court* I could not guarantee that the dialogue was exactly as I described it, because no matter how good your memory is, you cannot remember each spoken word. I forget things, I forget millions of things, but I would say that while other people may forget their childhood, I remember my childhood better than many things which happened to me in my ripe years. Not only do I remember facts but I remember images, I remember faces, I remember the way people spoke. When I write their dialogue, although it may not be correct, it's characteristic of the way they spoke.

BURGIN: How do these images come to you? Do you feel them first visually?

SINGER: Yes, visually. I dream about my childhood, although there is a certain kind of amnesia involved with dreams. When I first wake up, I remember my dreams but the images keep evaporating. If I would write down my dreams the moment I wake up, I could keep certain parts of them. I dream about my childhood, I see people who died God knows how many years ago. I create in my dreams all kinds of situations, very often embarrassing ones. Sometimes I'm astonished how negative my dreams are. I'm always in a kind of mess. Although I make a living now, in my dreams I'm poor. And I always try to write something and don't succeed. I write a novel which I cannot finish, I write a story and I get lost. I sometimes wonder why the power of dreaming puts me into these dilemmas. Sometimes I feel that the master of dreams is giving me warnings: "You remember these things which happened to you? They may happen again, be careful."

BURGIN: I imagine your dreaming also carries over into the daytime.

SINGER: Yes, I'm a daydreamer. I was a daydreamer when I was a child and in this respect I haven't changed at all. I'm daydreaming now in the ridiculous way that I did when I was seven or eight years old. In a way, some of my stories grow out of these dreams. While I forget my night dreams, I remember my daydreams more or less because they keep repeating themselves and there is a kind of system in them.

Literature is actually a form of daydreaming, under control or with a purpose. Not with a message, but with a purpose.

BURGIN: Your father gave you some advice, I think it was in *In My Father's Court*, where he said to be straightforward in your writing, to avoid casuistry, and "torturing the text." Did this advice influence you?

SINGER: My father spoke about religious literature but it influenced me very much in my secular writing because although I'm not a realist, I still don't believe in distorting things. There are a number of writers now who think that when they distort reality, it may magnify their power. Distortion is not the ideal of literature, because deep in his heart every writer wants to tell the truth. He is, in a way, a carrier of the truth, but he carries the truth in his own way, according to his emotions. A writer who will sit down and distort reality arbitrarily will never succeed from a literary point of view. When you read Tolstoy you see that although he's dreaming, he's trying his best to make his dreams as convincing as possible. I feel that now there is a tendency in literature towards distorting the order of things, not to create great art but to be "original" through distortion. Distortion and originality have become synonyms, while actually they are very far from one another.

BURGIN: I was under the impression that in the beginning this advice of your father's was something that didn't make a strong impact on you, but that in later years you found great sense in it.

SINGER: No, it made an impression immediately. I immediately felt that here's a straightforward man. Of course, he was a believer and I didn't believe that every word written in the Talmud was given on Mount Sinai. But as far as writing is concerned, he showed me that there is a logic to everything. A human being cannot escape logic. The great artists were also great logicians. Consider the stories of Edgar Allan Poe. You may say, "What kind of logic is there in Edgar Allan Poe?" Great logic. It is true that he believed in apparitions, and miracles, but once this premise was made he constructed his story accordingly. But the writers who distort reality distort logic.

BURGIN: Can you name a writer in this instance?

SINGER: I would say that this is true about the people who try to imitate Kafka. I wouldn't say it about Kafka himself. Also, the people who try to imitate Joyce do this. I would say that Pinter is doing it. He will distort reality, not to create better art, but to appear highly original. Spinoza says in his *Ethics* that the order of ideas and the order of things are alike. There is a connection between literature, art, and philosophy, and even science, although it may seem like a loose connection. There is profound logic in the works of the masters. They say in Yiddish, "If you have said Aleph you have to say Beth." There is also some consistency even in dreams, although it is a strange kind of logic . . . a hidden logic.

BURGIN: If we might return to your early years, what are the qualities that you miss most from your childhood?

SINGER: I was brought up in a world where there was a certain kind of hope, a belief that God has created the world and has given us the Torah, and that the Torah points to us the way of life. These premises might not have been true, but once the people believed in them there was a way of life for them. I have been brought up in the categories of good and evil. Almost nothing was neutral. Either you did a *mitzvah* or you did an *averah* (sin). In our time now, this way of thinking has almost disappeared. This state of affairs has created a crisis, not only in the ethics of people, but in many other ways. Children are being brought up today thinking that there isn't such a thing as good and evil, that everything is relative. But men cannot function and grow with a completely neutral way of thinking. A morally neutral human being is a monster.

BURGIN: There is a well-known anecdote in *In My Father's Court* which a number of critics have commented on because it seems to reveal, on the surface at any rate, an attitude you had towards your parents. It deals with geese that are somehow shrieking after they are dead and your father attributes this to a miracle while your mother solves the problem by pulling out their windpipes. I wonder what your thoughts are about how your mother and father affected your view of things?

SINGER: The truth is, my father believed in authority. For him, if a man was a holy man, everything he said was right. But my mother felt that no matter who the man was, if he spoke nonsense, it's nonsense. In this respect I am like my mother. Now if you would tell me that Shakespeare said something about art which I consider false, I would say it doesn't make sense to me. Even though I'm ready to accept all kinds of possibilities—that there are ghosts and there are apparitions and there are phantoms—just the same, if a medium will come to me and say that he can call on Spinoza every time he extinguishes the lights, I will be more than skeptical.

BURGIN: Maybe you took the best from your mother and father.

SINGER: I am not going to boast about this. I idolized them, I loved them (although it is the custom now to say, "I hate my father, I hate my mother," which people who go to psychoanalysts often say). Of course, when you love you cannot be one hundred percent objective. But just the same, I would say that I see their inconsis-

8

tencies and their mistakes—I do see them. I forgive them these mistakes because they existed for generations. As a matter of fact, as a boy, although I loved my parents dearly, I criticized them severely.

BURGIN: Would they ever speak to you about sexual matters, or was that a taboo subject?

SINGER: My parents believed, like all Jews, that if you marry a girl, if you go to the Rabbi and he marries you, then you are allowed to sleep together to produce children. If you give in to passion and break the law, you are on the way to perdition.

BURGIN: No premarital sex?

SINGER: Oh, God forbid. That was considered lechery in our house, although according to the strict Jewish law you have committed adultery only if you lived with a married woman. If you live with a woman who is not married, it's not really adultery.

BURGIN: Let me ask you a bit more about your family. I know you have the highest regard for your older brother.*

SINGER: Oh, I have great respect and love for him.

BURGIN: More so than for your father?

SINGER: No, I wouldn't say this. But I respected him as a human being, an excellent journalist, and a very good

* Israel Joshua Singer, the well-known novelist.

writer. He pointed the way to me. Many things which he told me I still admire today.

BURGIN: Such as?

SINGER: That a writer should not be an interpreter, that he should not try to explain the facts of life. He should only describe them, make them as alive as possible.

BURGIN: Over what things did you disagree?

SINGER: He was less a believer in the supernatural than I was. He really was, for a certain number of years, a rationalist. I often said to him, "We don't know nature," and to me nature is everything. The supernatural is also nature. I can still believe that there is a soul and there may be demons. Three hundred years ago people did not know about microbes and now they know that they exist. When it comes to the bare facts, logic cannot do anything about them—you have to use experience. You have to verify them.

BURGIN: What I'd like to find out finally about your childhood are those memories or impressions that are a permanent part of your sense of things.

SINGER: I would say my years in Warsaw were my most important years.

BURGIN: When were you there?

SINGER: Between 1908 and 1917. I keep going back to 10 Krochmalna Street in my writing. I remember every little corner and every person there. I say to myself that just as other people are digging gold which God has created billions of years ago, my literary gold mine is this street. I keep on returning to it with the feeling that there are still treasures which I haven't used up. Many writers have done the same before me. I have seen Knut Hamsun going back to the same people in almost all his works. It is true that I also write about later years, I even write about things which happened in the United States. But somehow it is easier for me to go back to these years in Warsaw than to any other time. They are to me a collection of human character . . . I describe the underworld there, too. As a rule I hate criminals, but somehow I can forgive those I knew when I was young because I saw the circumstances under which these creatures were brought up. It's easier for me to think with some tolerance about these lawbreakers of former times than about those of today.

BURGIN: You once made a remark that "in literature, as in our dreams, death does not exist."

SINGER: There's no question about it. Take, for example, the case of *Anna Karenina.* This book was written more than a hundred years ago but you don't say "the late Anna Karenina" or "the late Madame Bovary" or "the late Flaubert." They are alive. If the writer manages to imbue them with life, then they, together with their author, live forever. When people ask me, "Why do you write about a vanished world?" I answer, "Whether a hero is alive today and will be dead twenty years from now, or whether he died twenty years ago— or two thousand years ago—if the writer has given him life, he or she will be a living part of human consciousness."

BURGIN: You always wanted to write, as far back as you can remember . . .

SINGER: I would say from about sixteen.

BURGIN: And before then?

SINGER: There was a time when I wanted to be a scholar . . .

BURGIN: A rabbinical scholar?

SINGER: No. I wanted to become a doctor of medicine, a scientist, or perhaps a philosopher.

BURGIN: Why is it that, as the son and grandson of Rabbis, you never considered following that life?

SINGER: Because a Rabbi's life was in my eyes a miserable kind of life. First of all, a Rabbi preaches things which he has to believe in all his life and tries also to make other people believe. Since I was a skeptic about religion, I felt that for me to preach these things to others was absolutely wrong. In addition, a Rabbi is always criticized by his congregation. He has a lot of adversaries, and whatever happens, he's inevitably blamed. I've spoken to many Rabbis, even here in this country where the people don't demand so much from them. The life of a Rabbi is not to be envied and he's never really left in peace. It seldom happens in America that the son of a Rabbi also becomes a Rabbi, although it happens . . . But in the old country, this was almost the rule, because fathers compelled their sons to follow in their footsteps. In fact, every third Jew in Poland was a Rabbi. This is my impression now . . .

BURGIN: Did your father want you to follow him?

SINGER: Yes, he wanted that very much. But my younger brother followed him instead.

BURGIN: Did your father feel a sense of betrayal because you and your older brother became writers?

SINGER: Not only that we didn't want to be Rabbis, but that we left, from his point of view, our religion. From my father's perspective I was an atheist, even though I believed in God. But he demanded more. I had to believe in every little dogma and bylaw the Rabbis created generation after generation. I had to believe that they were all given to Moses on Mount Sinai. However, I could see that all these laws were man-made. For example, one law in the Bible became eighteen laws in the Mishnah and seventy in the Gemara or in the Book of Maimonides. This was their form of creativity. Just as the critics today will take a poem by Byron or Shelley and will write whole books about it, and they'll find in its verses things which the author never intended, so did our Rabbis use the words of the Torah. They had to be creative, they had to do something with their minds, and after a while the Jewish people had to live according to this hairsplitting. They made life so difficult that a religious Jew had no time for anything else but religion. It became for the Hassidim and for many other Jews a twenty-four-hour-a-day job. I could see this when I was still very young. I also asked myself questions: If there is a God, why is it that those who pray and carry all these man-made burdens are often poor and sick and miserable and those who don't practice them are often happy? I saw at a very early age that this kind of religion is nothing but commentary upon commentary, sheer casuistry.

BURGIN: Did your older brother influence you in your thinking about that?

SINGER: Yes, I heard his discussions with my parents. I would listen to him, and all his arguments were very strong, while the arguments of my parents seemed to me weak. All they could do was become angry and call him names. Now, my younger brother, Moishe, as you know, became a Rabbi and immensely pious. He became everything my father wanted him to be.

BURGIN: I understand your sister* was also a writer.

SINGER: My sister also wrote in Yiddish, but she did not succeed as much as her brothers, although she was not a bad writer. She was better than some of the so-called Yiddish talents of today.

BURGIN: You seem to be exploring your childhood memories again in your novel *Shosha.*

SINGER: In *Shosha* I wrote about 1911 and although I was a child then, I remember thousands of things—the way of life and how people looked and spoke. Their

* Hinde Esther Singer

Yiddish was rich in words and idioms and I remember that, too. There is something about writers—the first fifteen years of their life is never lost to them. It is like a well which is never exhausted.

BURGIN: Since you have such vivid memories of your early years, I wonder if you remember any childhood dreams.

SINGER: As a young man I had a dream that kept on repeating itself. I went somewhere, to a library or to a Jewish study house, and there I found an old book, which was both my book and somebody else's, written in very small letters, and I read it and it was full of wonderful stories. And while I read it I thought about taking it home, borrowing the book from the library. Sometimes I did take it home and I always felt that this was the kind of book I wanted to write and hadn't yet written. Sometimes I still see this book in my dreams, and the stories in it are queer and wondrous. Somewhere I still hope to both find this book and write it.

2.

First impressions of America . . . An artist, like a horse, needs a whip . . . Half Yasha, half Herman . . . On Kafka and a friend of Kafka . . . Small fish swim in schools

BURGIN: I wonder what your impressions of America were when you arrived in 1935.

SINGER: When I came to America I had a feeling of catastrophe. I ran away from one catastrophe in Poland and I found another one when I came here. I had been working in Warsaw as a Yiddish journalist, but the situation of the Jews in Poland became worse from day to day. Hitler was already in power in 1935 and the Nazis used to come to Poland to visit, to go hunting, and to talk to some of the Polish political leaders. My only hope was to come to America. I foresaw that there would be no rest in Poland. Many people were too optimistic or blind to see the danger. I foresaw the holocaust. Some people did foresee it but were unable to leave. Whatever the case, I had a strong hope that when I came to America I would see all these things which American propaganda described.

BURGIN: When you arrived in America you must have felt lost as far as your writing was concerned.

SINGER: I felt lost from many points of view.

BURGIN: Were either of your parents alive at this time?

SINGER: My mother was still alive; my older brother was in New York. My first impression was that Yiddish was in a very bad condition and it was not going to last in America more than another ten years. In 1935 it was the only language I spoke, although I knew Hebrew and also some Polish and German. I felt that I had been torn out of my roots and that I would never grow any new ones in this country. Almost all the young people I met were Communists. They spoke about Comrade Stalin as if he were not only the Messiah but the Almighty Himself, and I knew that it was all a big lie. Also I could not make a living here. The *Jewish Daily Forward* published some of the stories I brought with me but my desire for writing had evaporated. I was in a very bad state. In addition, in Warsaw I had women. Here I had difficulties in making acquaintances. The girls all spoke English and those who spoke Yiddish were too old and not exactly to my taste. Sex and Yiddish don't always go hand in hand.

My brother, of course, wanted to help me in every way but I just didn't want his help because I felt I'm already a man of thirty and it's time I was responsible for myself. I didn't want to become a *schnorrer* for the rest of my life.

BURGIN: Had you written any books by then?

SINGER: The only thing I had published in Poland was *Satan in Goray,* and also a few stories which I rejected later because I didn't like them anymore. I only allowed one story that I wrote in Poland to be translated into English. It is called "The Old Man."

I began life here in furnished rooms and I ate in cafeterias. After a while I found a better room and I found a girlfriend, although she was older than I. She was a most charming woman, a wonderful person.

BURGIN: A period of something like five years went by before you could write any fiction?

SINGER: Maybe seven or eight years. I came in 1935 and I began to write fiction again in about 1943. In the meantime, I did publish a number of articles and little sketches in the *Forward*. In 1943 they published *Satan in Goray* in New York with a few of the new stories. So after eight years I published an old book, a book which had already been printed, in addition to three or four new stories. I had the feeling then that my lot was to be one of those writers who write one book and become silent forever. There are such writers. But I said to myself that even if a writer writes one book which makes sense, he's still a writer. The question was: how would I make a living? I certainly could not make a living from this single book in Yiddish. When they published *Satan in Goray* again here in Yiddish, with a few new stories, my honorarium was ninety dollars. This went on until I began to publish more in the *Forward* . . . I still was not a member of the staff. They were not in a rush to take me, although they considered me a useful writer and they published me more than any other journalist. They published me a lot, but they paid me like a free-lancer.

BURGIN: When did you marry?

SINGER: I met Alma in 1937, and between meeting and marrying her three years went by. I loved her and she loved me but there were all kinds of problems. I couldn't make a living for myself, so how could I make a living for a wife? Also, since she was German (Jewish, of course), Alma didn't know Yiddish. I told her that I was a writer but I couldn't prove it. Nothing was yet translated. She had to believe me. In reality, I considered myself a has-been writer, an ex-writer, a writer who had lost both the power and the appetite for writing.

BURGIN: It must have been quite painful for you.

SINGER: Since I'm a pessimist, it's very easy for me to resign myself. I said, "In what way do I deserve better than all the other Jews in Poland? They are in the concentration camps." It's easy for me to resign myself. For me my personal life is always: "If it goes, it goes. If it doesn't go, it's too bad." I don't cry on anybody's shoulder. I wouldn't even cry on my own shoulder. But then suddenly, in the middle forties, the desire to write came upon me again and since then it has never really left.

BURGIN: How do you account for this? Did something stabilize in your situation?

SINGER: First of all, I got more or less used to New York; I learned a little English. When I arrived, I knew three words: "Take a chair." When I got on a bus, I didn't know how to tell the man where I wanted to go.

BURGIN: How did you survive here?

SINGER: Many people came here without knowing English. Do you think that the millions of immigrants who came here knew English?

BURGIN: Your English is impressive now. Was it a great struggle to learn it?

SINGER: I got a teacher here, a nice girl by the name of Mona Shub, who taught me English, and I also learned some on my own. I bought cards and I wrote a word on each card as if I would be an author of a dictionary, and every night before I went to sleep I repeated them. I also tried to read the Bible in English.

After a year I was able to make myself understood. I could even flirt with my teacher. My desire to learn English was very strong. I knew that if I didn't learn this language I would be lost forever. Immigrants seldom really learn English thoroughly, except such a master of language as Nabokov. Of course, I never intended to write in English. I knew that I would write in Yiddish all my life.

BURGIN: I once heard you describe Yiddish as being a very sensuous language.

SINGER: I would not say sensuous, but very rich in describing character and personality, though very poor in words for technology.

BURGIN: Did it ever occur to you to write in Polish?

SINGER: Not really.

BURGIN: You didn't see any advantage in terms of your career?

SINGER: Listen, what was Polish in America? Also a provincial kind of language.

BURGIN: Americans have been conditioned to think of careers in terms of a big break. I suppose it's part of our Hollywood complex. So I almost feel compelled to ask you if you ever got this "big break" in your writing life.

SINGER: The truth is, I never got a big break.

BURGIN: Well, you must have gotten something somewhere along the line.

SINGER: I never got it; neither did I expect it. Between 1935, when I came here, and 1945 I accomplished very little. Then in 1945 I suddenly began to write *The Family Moskat* for the *Forward*. I was already an old forgotten writer then, because when you are forty-one, and you have published one little book, you are completely out of it. I considered myself a journalist, not a writer. But then I began to write *The Family Moskat* and it was serialized in the *Forward* every week.

BURGIN: What kind of circulation does that paper have?

SINGER: It still has thirty thousand, maybe less. All the readers read my novel in the *Forward* because it's a small paper, with only about ten or twelve pages. People who buy it read almost everything in it. The man who was then the secretary of the *Forward*, Mr. Dan

Feder, went to Alfred Knopf on his own initiative and offered him *The Family Moskat.* Knopf wasn't interested since it was not translated into English. But this secretary managed to get a contract for me and an advance of five hundred dollars. And then about 1947, after publishing a lot of articles, I had saved enough money to go to Europe. I took a trip with Alma. We went to England and to France and to Switzerland. It was a big adventure because I took out every penny which I had saved, leaving here in the bank only about ten dollars. I mentioned Switzerland in *The Family Moskat* and I wanted to know how it looked. Knopf had a friend, Maurice Samuel, who had a friend named Abba Gross. Gross had translated a number of books before and he was out of work. Somehow all these people together made Knopf give me a contract and the advance. My brother, I. J. Singer, had published all his works at Knopf's and I was not a complete stranger to him.

BURGIN: Did there come a time when you suddenly realized, "My God, I'm writing consistently now, day after day?"

SINGER: In the *Forward,* when you begin a novel, you have to finish it. People were waiting, so every week I had to deliver "copy."

BURGIN: Do you still serialize your work in the *Forward?*

SINGER: Whatever I write, I serialize. An artist, like a horse, needs a whip. I'm so accustomed to delivering some stuff every week that it has become almost my

second nature. Now let me tell you, I haven't missed a
week in all these years, except that I get four weeks'
vacation. But then I work harder than ever in prepar-
ing copy for after the vacation. Getting back to *The
Family Moskat*. When the book was finally translated, it
was too large and I myself saw that it was far from being
right . . . I repeated many things and I missed many
things. I worked on this book another two years—editing, cutting, and adding a number of chapters. I worked
on it until it became as it is today. And then at the
beginning of 1950 the book came out in both Yiddish
and English and in a little while in Hebrew, too. This
might be what you call a break. I would say *The Family
Moskat* did it. And then about two years later, Saul
Bellow translated "Gimpel the Fool."

BURGIN: Where was that originally published?

SINGER: It was published first in Yiddish and my honorarium was twenty dollars. In 1952 it was published in
Partisan Review in English. At that time *Partisan Review* was read by all the intelligentsia, and by the writers, and for some reason this story gave me what I
would say was even more of a name than *The Family
Moskat*. Then another good thing happened in my life.
In 1953 or '54, I met Cecil Hemley. He was a small
publisher, the publisher of Noonday Press—he and Ar-
thur Cohen, who is now quite a well-known writer.
They published *Satan in Goray* in English, then
"Gimpel the Fool." These two books again got good
reviews. Irving Howe wrote a most favorable review
about *Satan in Goray*.

Since then I go on . . . still working.

BURGIN: I understand that when you came here you found the American character completely incomprehensible.

SINGER: It was difficult for me to understand their way of thinking.

BURGIN: What puzzled you?

SINGER: First of all, they were people born in a free country, they said what they wanted to say, and we were not accustomed to this in Poland. We were accustomed to people being very careful about what they were saying. Also, many things were foreign to me. I didn't know what stocks were, I didn't know what bonds were. To give you another example, in Poland if a man opened a store and the store was not a success he'd keep it going for years and years, always hoping. But here a man might open a store and four weeks later he'd close it. I saw millions of things here which astonished me just by their being different.

BURGIN: What about American women?

SINGER: American women looked to me very different, they used a language which people in Poland did not use.

BURGIN: Were they more aggressive in some ways?

SINGER: Yes, in a way aggressive, more aggressive and kind and humorous and silly. All I can say is they were very much different and I was prepared for it, because I knew that people *are* different. I know that if I went to

Mexico people would again be different from what I'm used to, and thank God that this is so. If people were all alike, there'd be no place for literature.

BURGIN: Aside from your personal troubles, what were your impressions of the country itself?

SINGER: I didn't know the country, but I loved New York. I loved it immensely. Then it was not like today. There was a spirit of freedom; there was no fear. The streets were full of life, I walked a lot, I felt free. I was sorry that Yiddish was neglected and I didn't like the idea that most of the people I met were Communists, but the city itself was exciting. And, of course, I was young, I got over my depression. Although I was poor, it never bothered me. I went to the library and I could read. I liked to go on the Fifth Avenue bus, which had an upper level, just to sit there and look at the city, or I made a trip on the El that went all over the city. To sit there and look out and see New York was a great adventure. Sometimes I took the ferry for a nickel and went to Staten Island. All these things for a poor man are big events. For five cents I made a trip on the ocean.

BURGIN: What do you think has been lost? What's happened to New York since then?

SINGER: There was never any fear in New York then. You could walk the streets. I was told you could even sleep in Central Park the whole night if it wasn't too cold. No one bothered you. You read in the newspapers sometimes about crime but it didn't happen often and people were gay, you know. New York was a gay city, almost as gay as Paris. And then, it began to deteriorate to such a degree that people now hide in their apartments like mice in holes. When I came here, there were many cafeterias; the cafeterias have also disappeared.

BURGIN: Why were you so fond of cafeterias?

SINGER: At that time, for thirty cents you could eat and sit the whole day long reading newspapers or books or even writing an article.

BURGIN: They never bothered you about leaving after you'd finished your meal?

SINGER: It never occurred to anybody to drive out a customer. In the beginning I thought that everything was expensive because I counted everything in zlotys, but then I realized that everything was actually cheaper here. I paid four dollars a week rent, although for me to pay these four dollars every week was a real crisis, but somehow I managed. Then I met a landsman from Bilgoray, and I moved into his house. After a while (you will not believe me) I had three furnished rooms; one was in my landsman's house in Brooklyn, where I didn't pay rent at all, one I had on Seventieth Street, where I paid four or five dollars a week, and one was in Seagate in Brooklyn. I had one girlfriend in Manhattan and one in Brooklyn.

BURGIN: Could this possibly have formed part of the basis of the novel *Enemies, A Love Story?*

SINGER: It may be something like that . . . I lived in three rooms and my rent was about nine dollars a week altogether, since one room I got free.

BURGIN: I find this funny because Herman Broder in *Enemies, A Love Story* is by far the most passive of your main characters.

SINGER: Yes.

BURGIN: He seems to basically let things happen to him.

SINGER: Yes, this is true.

BURGIN: Maybe that was the feeling you had about yourself at that time.

SINGER: It's true about me all my life. It's true even today.

BURGIN: But if you compare a Herman Broder, who was juggling different women, to Yasha in *The Magician of Lublin,* who was doing the same thing, you see that Yasha is more active. He's trying, in effect, to play God, to maneuver events like a magician manipulating his wares.

SINGER: I would say I am half Yasha, half Herman. Yes, I'm kind of passive. I never went after women, they had to come to me because I was shy. I would say that Herman is what I really was and Yasha is maybe what I wanted to be. I don't think I ever stretched out my hand for anything. I never wrote a letter to anybody. I never asked any favors. If someone wrote to me, maybe I answered, maybe not, but I never sent anything to a publisher or to a magazine.

BURGIN: Why, do you suppose?

SINGER: I don't know. I'm born sort of proud. I'm something of a fatalist. I believe that what is destined will come to me. I would probably have gotten much more if I had gone after love, money, recognition, but it's not in my nature to take any action except in my work. My only battlefield is my desk or lap on which I write. There I fight with phrases, with words, but with people I'm very, very passive.

BURGIN: During this time you weren't able to write because of all the understandable complications and problems you had. But was there a certain day when you realized, "I can sit down, I'm at peace, I can write . . ."?

SINGER: "Certain days" only happen in stories. There never is a "certain day" in life, only uncertain days and even less certain nights.

BURGIN: You mean it was a gradual thing.

SINGER: Gradual, and with interruptions. Also I married Alma in 1940 and I suddenly had a real home. And then my work increased at the *Forward*.

BURGIN: Do you still write for the *Forward* mainly out of a sense of loyalty?

SINGER: I like this discipline. I know that without it I would postpone things.

BURGIN: Do you ever feel that you may be writing too fast because you're under pressure to constantly deliver material?

SINGER: Yes, I write fast, but then I rewrite. There were also a number of cases where I did not succeed. I don't have these pieces translated. I let them stay in Yiddish, and I hope that no one is going to translate them after my death.

BURGIN: Like Kafka?

SINGER: There is no Max Brod in my life. I hope my heirs will respect this wish. I cannot *burn* my manuscripts. They are published.

BURGIN: Speaking of Kafka, you entitled one of your collections of stories *A Friend of Kafka* and the title story is one of your better-known stories—Do you have a special interest in him or was that just a literary conceit?

SINGER: There was a man in Warsaw called Jacques Levy, whom Kafka mentions in his diary many times. He was a Yiddish actor. As you know, Yiddish theater came to Prague in 1911 and this Jacques Levy was one of the main actors there. A Yiddish actress named Madame Tschissik also came to Prague at this time and Kafka fell in love with her. This man whose name was Jacques Levy (I changed the name to Jacques Cohen in my story) used to talk to me about Kafka, the great

Kafka, and how Kafka kept writing letters to him, and I said, "Who the hell is this Kafka?" and he said, "One day you will know. He will one day be famous." I thought he invented the man.

BURGIN: When did this happen?

SINGER: This was in the early twenties. This Madame with whom Kafka was supposed to be so much in love looked to me like a middle-aged, unattractive woman.

BURGIN: Kafka said everything in metaphors anyway.

SINGER: Maybe she was a beautiful metaphor, then. Anyway, I actually learned about Kafka years later. I believe that Kafka was a potential genius, but I don't think he really succeeded in everything. Some of his things are very good and some of his things bore me. It is the custom in this country always to mention Kafka and Dostoyevsky in one breath as if they were Siamese twins.

BURGIN: Personally I wouldn't say that at all.

SINGER: I agree. The truth is, Dostoyevsky was a first-class genius who will most probably last much longer than Kafka. Kafka has created a new kind of trend, a fashion, but as far as the mastery of writing is concerned, he's much below Dostoyevsky.

BURGIN: What are the works of his that you feel are successful?

SINGER: Well, he succeeds in some stories like "The Metamorphosis." He succeeded in other works, too. The spark of greatness is everywhere, but his book *Amerika* I don't like at all. Since the strength of his books is in symbolism, they strike me as too long. Symbols must be short.

BURGIN: Like *The Trial* or *The Castle* . . .

SINGER: They go on, they drag on. I feel in Kafka, as I said, a great power, but the truth is that the literary idols of this generation are not my idols—neither Kafka nor Joyce. I have to make an effort to read them and I don't think that fiction is good when you have to make an effort. After you read, say, fifty pages of *The Trial,* you get the point. I see already that we will never know what the crime is, so I'm not as hot about Kafka or about Joyce as most people are. I'm not even so hot about Proust. He's written eighteen volumes about his family, it's too much. I think that there should be a law that no book should be larger than a thousand pages. I don't believe in forced reading, where students are forced by professors or they compel themselves to read. Since I believe that literature is basically entertaining, the quantity is as important as the quality. A play of ten acts is a bore even if it is good. We must enjoy art. No commentary or footnote should explain our pleasure. It is true that there are vulgar readers who enjoy kitsch but the enjoyment of kitsch is better, in my eyes, than the masochism of the reader who reads out of duty or to adjust himself to some vogue of art. It is also true that the great writers were all sufferers but they never wanted the reader to suffer—the very opposite, they wanted him or her to forget their troubles while they read. We have now a whole bevy of writers who take pride in annoying the reader. They make him feel guilty and bore him. They weep on the reader's shoulder and this is proclaimed the very mission of the so-called serious writer. The great writers always gave joy to the readers even in their tragedies. Kafka, Joyce, and Proust are great talents, but Kafkaism, Joyceism, and even Proustism have become a burden to young students. The fact is that all "isms" are bad for literature. Every "ism" is by its very definition a cliché. In literature and in art generally all schools and disciples are bad. The various schools and "isms" of literature were invented by professors. Tolstoy didn't belong to any school. Only small fish swim in schools.

3.

Sex and contact with humanity . . . The
cult of personality . . . Two kinds of readers
. . . A spiritual dictatorship

BURGIN: You told me that you consider yourself a kind
of recluse, yet you're constantly seeing people and entertaining them.

SINGER: I used to be a recluse.

BURGIN: You mean when you first came to America.

SINGER: When I first came to America, I was kind of a
recluse. There are two powers in me. One power tells
me to go away somewhere—to an island—and hide
from this whole abomination and cruelty. "Don't ever
see another human being, lock yourself up and live like
a misanthrope." And another power tells me to accept
people, talk to them. There is a struggle all the time
within me. I also know that if I stay away from people,
then I have to deal with only one human being—myself
—and I'd rather have other people than to all the time
have only myself for an associate. When you are with
yourself your egotism grows, your bitterness and suspi-
cions grow. You become twice as *meshuga* as before.

BURGIN: How do you reconcile these two opposing needs or compulsions?

SINGER: A man must have some contact with humanity, whether he wants it or not. I would say that the best contact with humanity is through love and sex. Here, you learn many things about life, because in sex and in love human character is revealed more than anywhere else. Let's say that a man in society can play a very strong man, a dictator, but in sex he may become reduced to a child, or to an imp. The sexual organs are the most sensitive organs of the human being. For example, the eye or the ear never sabotage you. An eye will not stop seeing if it doesn't like what it sees, but the penis will stop functioning if it doesn't like what it "sees." I would say that the sexual organs express the human soul more than any other part of the body. They are not diplomats. They tell the truth ruthlessly. It's nice to deal with them and their caprices, but they are even more *meshuga* than the brain.

BURGIN: After your period of isolation ended and your career developed you must have had contact with a number of writers.

SINGER: No, I didn't. When I was young I used to read books and I never really looked at who the author was. I didn't care. When I was a boy of twelve, I read Tolstoy, but I didn't know it was Tolstoy. I didn't even know that I was reading a translation. What's the difference? I was interested in the story, not the author. I could not repeat the word Dostoyevsky. I didn't care because a real reader, especially a young reader, never cares too much about the author. On the other hand, the academic reader doesn't really care about the story; he cares about the author. We are living now in a time when people are so interested in the author that the story is almost secondary, which is very bad. Many of the readers of today themselves want to be writers. They are interested in the shop; they are interested in the maker. The good reader, the real reader when he is young, doesn't care so much who Tolstoy was and what he was. He wants to read the book and he enjoys it.

BURGIN: Is this why you enjoy writing for children so much?

SINGER: Children are wonderful because they are completely independent readers. A child would not read a book because it was written by a "great writer" —a man with great authority. The fact that Shakespeare has written it will not impress a child—the child will look over the story by himself and see if he likes it or not. You cannot impress a child by criticism. You cannot say, "This is a wonderful book because such and such critic has said it's wonderful." A child doesn't care about the critics, because the child himself is a critic. A child will not read a book because it was advertised in a very big way. He is actually a more independent reader than the adult, who is impressed by authorities, criticism, and big advertisements in the New York *Times* or on television. It's harder to fool children than to fool adults when it comes to literature.

To repeat: When people begin to be less interested in art, they become more interested in the artist and vice versa. What I say may seem false to you.

BURGIN: No, quite the contrary.

SINGER: Now, notice how many books come out about Hemingway. In the olden times they wouldn't have written so many books about a writer. They would read him and say whether it's a good story or a bad story, whether they are interested or not. But people have become more interested in Hemingway the man than in what Hemingway has written. There are many people who have read books about Hemingway without reading Hemingway, and this is true about other writers and it's true about artists. Take the famous painter in Paris, the greatest, who died not long ago . . . the creator of modernism, Picasso. When people buy a picture, it has to be a Picasso. It's Picasso's name they're interested in. Sometimes the painting itself doesn't make any impression on the customer, but it is important that it was done by Picasso. This has become the curse of literature, too. When literature and art become overly "erudite" and develop a cult of personality, it means that the interest in art is gone and the artist has become a kind of idol.

BURGIN: What you say seems true to me. But if, let's say, you had a chance to meet Tolstoy, wouldn't that interest you or excite you?

SINGER: The truth is, if Tolstoy lived across the street, I wouldn't try to go see him. I would rather read what he writes.

BURGIN: You wouldn't be curious to meet him face to face?

SINGER: Not really . . . I've heard people make such a fuss, for instance, about the possibility that Shakespeare did not write his plays. What is the difference *who* wrote them?

BURGIN: And you wouldn't be curious to meet Shakespeare if you could?

SINGER: Not at all. You see, I don't care if his work was written by Bacon or by some ghost writer. Let the professors worry. I am still a reader. When you are really hungry, you don't look for the biography of the baker.

BURGIN: It does seem that society's current fascination with the "cult of personality" has become a kind of fetish.

SINGER: For example, people will read scores of books about Jesus Christ and debate whether he really existed. While the interest in what Christ has taught is becoming smaller, the curiosity about the man is growing. There is a reverse proportion in this. The less you are interested in a discipline or in a lore, the more you are interested in the creator of this lore, its development, its story.

BURGIN: Much of what you say seems obviously true. In fact, real writers wouldn't write if they felt that they would be considered more important than their works. They want to be lost in their works; they want their works to be more important than they are.

SINGER: Do you know that in his time I'm sure many people read Dickens, but I don't think there were two books written about him while he was alive. When people go to see a play by Pinter, many times they are more interested in Pinter than in his play. Sometimes the only good thing about the play is that Pinter has written it. Tell them it was not written by Pinter, but by Sminter, and they would immediately leave the theater. The worship of the trademark has become so important that the merchandise is becoming almost valueless. I think these things should be emphasized because they are at the very root of the crisis of all values in our time. It's true about religion, it's true about art, it's true about politics, and it's becoming true about everything. This is a kind of spiritual system of dictatorship where the authority is everything and the idea is nothing. It is not an accident that the pious Jews knew almost nothing about the life of their prophets, the creators of the Talmud, or their many saints and spiritual leaders. They were interested in what those great men taught, not in whom they married and where they lived. While there are thousands and thousands of books about Jesus, I never read one single book about the life of Moses. Neither did my father. You may say they cared about the medicine, not about the person who prescribed it.

4.

The problem of comedy . . . America is
waiting for a Gogol . . . Floods of
propaganda . . . The Jews of Vilna

BURGIN: We've discussed many serious themes; I
thought we might talk a bit about comedy. First, what
do you understand comedy to be? What are its conditions, and how do you distinguish different types of
comedy?

SINGER: Bergson has written a book about humor, and
he came to the conclusion that when people act according to a certain routine or rules, without seeing the
exception, this is comedic. Let's consider the man who's
always polite, who always says, "It's nice to see you" or
"I hope to see you again." But if some day when he's
being arrested or being hanged he would say to the
executioner, "Nice to see you, I hope to see you again,
come up to see me sometime," it would be funny because he repeats himself like a parrot. This is Bergson's
theory, but, like all definitions, it does not cover everything. There are so many instances of humor! Actually
every act of foolishness evokes humor. A mother will
say to her child, "Don't behave in this way, people will
laugh at you." People laugh at fools. The question actually is not what is humor, but what is foolish. The psy-

chologists for some reason have never covered this. I have never heard any definition of a fool by a psychologist, because to know what a fool is, we would also have to define cleverness, and although we use these expressions all the time, they are things we can't clearly define. According to the Old Testament, a clever man is one who goes in the ways of God, and a fool is a sinner. This is the biblical definition, but there is more to it than this. I would say that a fool not only uses clichés in his talk but acts according to clichés. His whole behavior is a cliché. Comedy is created when you let people be extremely banal. But I'm not sure that this covers the whole thing either.

BURGIN: What about the clever man who has wit? Aren't you leaving aside the question of wit in this definition of comedy?

SINGER: Whenever a person has wit, there's always a victim of this wit. He always makes fun of somebody, and it is always a human being. You don't say that a dog is funny or a horse is funny. No one will say that a rock or a river is funny. If you say that a table is funny, you make fun of the carpenter who made the table. Actually, humor is a criticism of human behavior. When we say that someone is a fool, we imply that he has free will, that he could have acted in a clever way if he had made an effort. Here humor and ethics meet. If we assume that a man is completely predetermined and has to act the way he acts, then we can't call him foolish or immoral, just as we wouldn't criticize animals or stones with such terms. Humor and wit are ways of characterizing people and their refusal to learn, to go deeper into matters, to see with their own eyes instead of with someone else's, or not to see at all.

BURGIN: Can you give me an example of a fool from your work?

SINGER: Gimpel the Fool is an example.

BURGIN: You find him a comedic character?

SINGER: He is funny, although we pity him. His wife Elka sleeps with all the other men, but he refuses to see it to such a degree that when he comes home at night and finds the apprentice in bed with his wife and she tells him, "Go out and see how the goat is doing," he "forgets" all about the discovery he just made and goes out, and when he comes back the apprentice is gone. He actually believes people to such a degree that he stops being himself.

BURGIN: Can you name any other characters whom you consider among the funniest in your work?

SINGER: I don't remember anyone in particular in *Satan in Goray* who would make you laugh. In *The Family Moskat* there are some funny types, old-fashioned people who act in a comedic way.

BURGIN: What about your other epic, *The Manor* and *The Estate?* For example, Mirkin is kind of a fool. Do you find him a humorous character?

SINGER: To a degree.

BURGIN: Maybe he's too grotesque or manipulative to be funny.

SINGER: He's ridiculous in the way he pursues Clara. Actually, the definition of the Bible is in a way right, that whenever a man does not act in the right way he is foolish . . . Still, we wouldn't laugh at Hitler, because he did so many malicious things that we are not in the mood to laugh. To laugh at someone is also to admit that the man is kind of innocent or helpless.

BURGIN: You've lived half your life in one culture and half your life in another. Do you find that there is something in the American character, as you've been able to perceive it, which makes for a different sense of humor than, say, Polish or Yiddish humor?

SINGER: I feel that America is waiting for a Gogol or a Sholem Aleichem, because behavior in this country has become so standardized that we are slowly losing our sense of human values. It is a result of the fact that the media are so omnipresent in this country. We are fooled by myriads of generalizations and by floods of propaganda.

BURGIN: Where do you find this American standardization which results in humor?

SINGER: The American way of trying to buy friendship, to solve all problems with money, is humorous. Give the Italians so much money and they will love us. If there is too much promiscuity in this country, the prescription is ready-made: we should spend a few billion dollars to put an end to promiscuity. If we had an

American humorist, he would be misunderstood, because most of the critics are liberals and they would never allow anyone to make fun of a liberal. Actually, the American liberal would be the best material for a humorist, because of his clinging to so many clichés. And of course, extreme conservatism can also be ridiculous. In the television discussion between Carter and Ford, suddenly Ford began to say that Poland is a real democracy. Here is a ridiculous thing; for no reason whatsoever Ford said that Poland and Czechoslovakia are completely free countries . . .

BURGIN: He made a mistake, yes.

SINGER: But it's a silly mistake. Whatever his opponent said, he had to say the opposite. Since Carter for a moment seemed anti-Russian, Ford had to be pro-Russian. It made people laugh because here is this conservative man who is so often defending the conservative ideals, and suddenly he emerges as an advocate of Communistic "democracy."

BURGIN: What comic characteristics do you find among the people you know best, the Jews?

SINGER: Jewish social activists believe that anti-Semitism can be overcome by petitions, by protests. They go out on Fifth Avenue and have a demonstration against anti-Semitism. There's always this silly belief that you can force or pay people to love you. In this respect Jews all over the world think and act like Americans.

BURGIN: Are there any other qualities besides humor that you find different in the American sensibility, if one may use such a term?

SINGER: Americans are perhaps more easily hypnotized than other human beings, and I don't mean by a man who sits there and says you are falling asleep. What I mean is hypnotized by fashions, by slogans, by clichés, by advertisements. The power which advertising and television has here is not only because the economy is greater but because the American is really gullible. I once spoke to a man who had a perfume factory and he said if you advertised urine on a whole page of a big newspaper as perfume, some readers would run and buy it, and believe it's perfume.

BURGIN: At the risk of sounding a trifle defensive about my country—don't you feel that trait is after all universal? Isn't it also true, for example, that Germany was hypnotized in a terrible way in the thirties?

SINGER: A great number of Germans believed in what Hitler preached even before Hitler emerged. They considered Germany above everything; the strongest and most privileged nation, a chosen people, a nation of supermen. Getting back to America, in no other country in the world will a man say, "I wear a three-hundred-dollar suit." He may boast that he wears a good suit by a famous tailor, but he will not mention the price.

BURGIN: That's typically American, it's true.

SINGER: It's also becoming European. More and more, money is becoming the measurement of human values in the capitalist countries—and power in the Communist. Of these two evils I prefer the first. It is less dangerous.

BURGIN: You were talking a bit about the comedic qualities in Jewish people. In *The Family Moskat* you said, "The Jews are a people who can't sleep themselves and let nobody else sleep." Can you elaborate?

SINGER: What I mean is that the Jew is such a restless creature that he must always do something, plan something . . . He is the kind of man who, no matter how many times he gets disappointed, immediately makes up some other illusions both for himself and for others.

BURGIN: You really think that's a special trait only of Jews?

SINGER: It's a special trait of intellectuals, but since the Jews are almost all actual or potential intellectuals, our restlessness and eagerness to do things has become almost a national trait. There is a story about a Jewish man who went to Vilna and when he came back he said, "This Vilna is the most unusual city. I have never seen any place like it. The Jews of Vilna are especially remarkable people." The other said, "What's so remarkable?" He said, "I saw there a Jew who all day long was scheming how to make money, how to get rich. I saw a Jew who's all the time waving the red flag and calling for revolution. I saw a Jew who was running after every woman and I saw a Jew who was an ascetic and preached religion all the time." The other man said, "I don't know why you are so astonished. Vilna is a big city, and there are many Jews there, all types." "No," said the first man, "it was the same Jew." In a way there is some truth in this story about the so-called worldly Jew. He is so restless that he is almost everything at once. When he gets an idea into his head it becomes so strong that he forgets about everything else. Let's consider the Jew who fights anti-Semitism. He will find anti-Semitism everywhere, even on an empty island or in the Sahara. The obsessed person becomes funny because he cannot see the exception to the rule, or he creates nonexistent rules. I would say that the great misfortune of literature and of life itself is the cliché, the generalization, while life itself has more exceptions than rules.

BURGIN: Maybe the rule is that life is full of exceptions.

SINGER: The axiom of art is that every moment of our existence is unique. The Jews are waiting for another Sholem Aleichem and America is waiting for a new Mark Twain or for an American Gogol. But I don't think that the American people would appreciate a really humorous book about themselves. They would say it's false, it's not accurate, it's contrived. This is also true about the modern Jews. If they had a Sholem Aleichem today, they would call him a Jewish anti-Semite. They would complain that he makes us look silly and that he helps our enemies. I speak about the modern Jew. The religious Jew has embraced the Bible, which keeps on upbraiding the Jew, calling him the worst kinds of names, predicting countless punishments for him. This shows the greatness of the historic Jew.

5.

The highest human entertainment . . .
Sexual modernism . . . Othello is not a man
of our times . . . The stream of
consciousness and the heresy of psychology
. . . Forced originality

BURGIN: You mentioned in an earlier conversation with me that you saw the main purpose of literature as being a form of entertainment. If that's so, what do you suppose it is that gives readers a sense of enjoyment from a book?

SINGER: When people come together—let's say they come to a little party or gathering—you always hear them discuss character. They will say, "This one is a fool, this one is a miser." Gossip makes the conversation. It seems that the analysis of character is the highest human entertainment. And literature does it, unlike gossip, without mentioning specific names—and so it is less malicious.

BURGIN: If we consider the proliferation of gossip columns in the newspapers and magazines and then consider the attitude that many people have towards them, it seems there's virtually a whole movement contending that literature is really an extension of gossip.

SINGER: Except with literature it's gossip without the damage which gossip does. When you make it anonymous, it doesn't do harm. At the same time you discuss character. The fiction writers who don't discuss character and only discuss social problems take away from literature its very essence. They stop being entertaining. We always love to discuss and reveal character because human character is to us the greatest puzzle. No matter how much you know a human being you don't know him enough. Discussing character constitutes a supreme form of entertainment.

BURGIN: I notice in looking over your work a special understanding of women, and I'm wondering if that's a quality you find lacking in many American novelists.

SINGER: If a man understands men, he also understands women and vice versa. I would not say there is a man who has a great understanding of men and no understanding of women. Most of the people understand almost no one except their business, and sometimes not even that.

BURGIN: And yet if you think of a writer we were just talking about yesterday—Dostoyevsky—you don't really remember many female characters particularly.

SINGER: Oh, yes. He has Sonya in *Crime and Punishment*.

BURGIN: Don't you think she is kind of a stereotype? A prostitute with a heart of gold.

SINGER: She's not a stereotype. The stereotype was made by those who imitated him.

BURGIN: Well, he initiated the stereotype, I suppose.

SINGER: The man who compared the eyes of his beloved girl to stars for the first time was highly original. Sonya is a living person. She's a three-dimensional person. She is sentimental, but sentimentality was a part of Russian life. Whores are known to be sentimental. She's a Russian character. And there is more, there are also Raskolnikov's mother and sister. They write a letter in *Crime and Punishment* which is just wonderful. True, Dostoyevsky makes them write this letter; it is true that as a rule people don't write letters like this, but it's great and revealing anyhow. No, I think he knew women.

BURGIN: Tolstoy is definitely a different case.

SINGER: I don't notice that Dostoyevsky writes mostly about men. In the theater you sometimes will see a play with six men around one or two women. In the theater also they prefer more men than women.

BURGIN: But not in your theater, the whole scope of your works.

SINGER: I often write about women, but always in relation to men.

BURGIN: I think your understanding of women is extremely impressive.

SINGER: Some women accuse me of hating women. The liberated woman propagandist suspects every man. Like a zealous Jew who often calls every Gentile an anti-Semite, the agitator of women's liberation calls every man an anti-feminist. They have created this kind of clannishness. They would like writers to write that every woman is a saint and a sage and every man is cruel and an exploiter. The moment a thing becomes an "ism," it is already false, and ridiculous.

BURGIN: You've talked about the unchanging qualities of people, but the situation of women has changed and you must have seen that happening in your lifetime, as well as the situation of many other people changing.

SINGER: I will tell you what I have seen. Jealousy, which people used to believe was a very strong instinct, for which they were ready to die and kill, has stopped playing the huge part which it played a century ago. Two great writers, Pushkin and Lermontov, died in duels because someone tried to spoil the reputation of their wives. People now have become less and less sensitive about this matter. A betrayed man does not feel anymore that he has been so wronged. Many men allow their women to have affairs and they don't make a fuss about it. And women even more so will tolerate this from men. I don't know how it happened, but this feeling that the other person is your property is slowly disappearing.

BURGIN: Does that disturb you or do you think it's healthy?

SINGER: In a way it disturbs me because I am accustomed to the old way. If my wife told me she had a lover, I would not stay with her another day. But at the same time I think there's something healthy about this change. I don't think humanity can exist now in the way it did centuries ago where the woman was the property of the man for life. Many people have made up their minds that they cannot make a contract for love to last a lifetime. More and more men and women have come to the conclusion that they cannot ask those who love them now for a guarantee of fidelity until they die. I still consider a monogamous love the *ideal*, but not all people are inclined to embrace this ideal.

BURGIN: I remember reading an essay by Bertrand Russell in a collection called *Skeptical Essays* where he said it should be mandatory for couples to live together for three years before they get married. Would you think that an intelligent law?

SINGER: Also to put in the marriage certificate that it's valid for, say, the next twenty years. When man and wife bring up their children, there must be faithfulness, because if not, no man would know if he's the father of the child or not. But the way it is in the New Testament that what God has joined no man can ever disjoin, this is an ideal not a reality. It seems to me that many people have decided that this cannot work. So although I myself would not practice sexual modernism, I believe that the changes which have taken place in sexual relations and love are not just fads, but a product of human development, and human nature.

BURGIN: So then there has been, if not exactly progress, certain dramatic changes.

SINGER: I don't know if I would call it progress, but a change has certainly come in my time, because when I was brought up people still believed in the same things about the family that they believed in five hundred years ago. *Anna Karenina*, although it's very much valid and still a wonderful work of fiction, is actually not a book of our times anymore, not completely so . . .

BURGIN: It's lost its shock value in many ways.

SINGER: The topic is becoming a little obsolete because the problem of conjugal loyalty is not treated anymore with such zeal and with such bitterness as in olden times. Othello is no longer a man of our times, or if he is, he's a remnant. Let me repeat something which may or may not have a connection with our conversation. Our discoveries in literature should not be so much in words, phrases, or style as in the new phases and new facets of human conduct. The writer who all the time ponders his style makes no discoveries. The real writer's gold mine is the outside world, its constant changes, its bizarre complications, the various human characters, man's passions, follies, errors, hopes, disappointments, especially in love. Tolstoy, Dostoyevsky, Balzac, Dickens, and Gogol didn't write about themselves all the time. They seldom wrote in the first person.

BURGIN: But don't you think Dostoyevsky really dramatized different aspects of himself in his characters, albeit often extraordinarily contradictory ones?

SINGER: Just the same, these writers investigated other characters and other situations. They did not play around all the time with their own moods and with their literary calligraphy. Dostoyevsky was not a murderer, but he wrote a book about a student, a murderer. You can say, of course, that he saw himself as Raskolnikov, but he contemplated other lives, other personalities, all the time. Although in life I am an introvert, I feel that in my writing I'm kind of an extrovert. A writer must be able to forget himself, at least for some of the time. Tolstoy does, but Proust doesn't.

BURGIN: How do you account for the fact that while society is becoming in many ways more extroverted, more open in terms of human relations, so much of literature is now so introspective?

SINGER: The Freudian theory—this business of analysis and pondering one's complexes—has made many people very curious about themselves, their inhibitions, and their caprices. The writers of the nineteenth century were also curious about themselves but they knew that the real power of literature is in observing other people. There's not a single story of Chekhov where he wrote about himself.

Although I do write from time to time in the first person, I don't consider it a healthy habit. I'm against the stream of consciousness because it means always babbling about oneself. The writer who writes about himself all the time must become a bore, just like the man who talks all the time about himself. When the writer becomes the center of his attention, he becomes a *nudnik*. And a *nudnik* who believes he's profound is even worse than just a plain *nudnik* (bore).

BURGIN: What about the so-called stream-of-consciousness technique used by Faulkner and Joyce in which there is more than one narrator?

SINGER: I don't think that they really made great stories. The truth is that we know what a person thinks, not by what he tells us, but by his actions. This reminds me—once a boy came to the *cheder* where I studied, and he said, "Do you know that my father wanted to box my ear?" So the teacher said, "How do you know that he wanted to box your ear?" And the boy said, "He did."

A man may sit for hours and talk about what he thinks, but what he really is, you can judge best by what he does. This is the real heresy in the psychoanalysis of our time where everything is measured by your thoughts and by your moods.

When you read the Bible, it never tells you what a man thought. It's always what he did. Take Genesis or the books of Joshua, Samuel, and Kings. David did this and Saul did this and Jonathan did this. There is one case in the Book of Esther where it says that "Haman said in his heart." So the Talmud says that this proves that the writer of the Book of Esther was inspired by the holy spirit, because if not, he would not have known what Haman was thinking in his heart. When you read Tolstoy and Flaubert and Chekhov, it's always what the hero or heroine said or did. I myself would never begin a story with, say, "Mr. So-and-So was sitting and thinking." I would rather describe how he looked, what he did and what he said. I would rather give a situation than just show his broodings. I know that there may be exceptions to the rule and I know that what I'm saying is not what is accepted today in literary criticism, but I say it just the same.

BURGIN: Perhaps one possible reason for the amount of inaction in much of contemporary literature, in terms of how you describe "action," is due to a feeling of impotence, a feeling that people can't, in any meaningful sense, "act" anymore.

SINGER: When you read a newspaper, you never find in the news what someone was thinking, but always his deeds. This is the reason why people read newspapers with so much more appetite than they read books. The paper tells you that a man has murdered his wife, not that he pondered about it. In many cases the reader already knows the psychology behind the deed. If you read that a man came home to his wife, he found her lover in her bed, and he shot both of them, you understand more or less how angry he was, and what he was thinking when he was arrested. Real literature concentrates on events and situations. The stream of consciousness becomes obvious very soon and therefore tedious. Tolstoy sometimes describes what his heroes were thinking and Dostoyevsky does this more often; nevertheless, their works are full of action and suspense. It's not the kind of false and contrived action which you'll find in kitsch novels, but there is action anyhow. When you read *Crime and Punishment* you don't know until the last page why Raskolnikov did what he did. We know how Raskolnikov *tries to explain it.* His talk is interesting because he doesn't talk to himself but to the district attorney.

The stream of consciousness is really a way of avoiding the story, of avoiding describing character. Also, it's a very easy method. You let a man talk for three hundred pages without revealing much. However, when it comes to exceptional talents, all these rules are not valid. A great talent can even give you a lot of revealing action within a stream of consciousness, but I don't think it has been done yet in a very convincing way. The so-called avant-garde writer always fails because he puts all his efforts into style, into a forced originality. He forgets or ignores the genuine originality of events, situations, or strange human encounters. He believes that by omitting punctuation, or by signing his name without capital letters, or by other tricks he becomes unique. Actually, these writers imitate one another all the time because the number of these devices is limited. They ultimately become banal, silly mannerisms. These writers are and remain stagnant and utterly boring, while life around them teems with action and novelty. By doing away with rhythm and rhyme, and by running away from narrative poetry, the modern poet has destroyed the market for poetry. He has become so obscure and so limited in his creativity that the reader has lost all interest in him and his puzzles.

6.

What is common to all is of no interest . . .
Jewish attachment to history . . .
Assimilation and writing . . . A spiritual
address

BURGIN: I'm wondering if you feel a writer has any special need of getting involved or committing himself in political or social affairs.

SINGER: It's unhealthy. I have never seen a single political novel or a single novel which has to do with sociology which really came out well. I will tell you why. Sociology doesn't deal with a single person or a few persons, but with masses of people, and in a way this is true about psychology. In *Crime and Punishment*, Dostoyevsky did not investigate the problem of crime generally, because there are very few criminals who are like Raskolnikov. Raskolnikov was meant to be a unique case. It is true that you can learn a little from the unique about the general, but this is not actually the artist's goal. In literature, what is common to all is of no interest. I once said that if Newton had really discovered gravitation by seeing an apple fall and gravitation was valid for this particular apple only, Newton wouldn't have become famous. It was by generalizing the case, by proving that this apple and a stone and the earth and the planets and all the bodies of the heavens have the same quality, that gravitation became such an important discovery. In literature it's the very opposite. If a real writer or painter wants to describe or paint an apple, it has to be a unique apple. Because of this, the moment the writer begins to dabble with generalizations or with the masses, he's already out of his profession.

For example, in *War and Peace*, there are only a few characters who are really interesting. We learn very little about Napoleon's wars. What we learn is about Andrei and Natasha and a few other people. When Pierre in *War and Peace* begins to make speeches about the agrarian question and how to free the peasants, it becomes such a bore that most of the readers skip it.

BURGIN: And in life, apart from literature, you don't feel a need to make a political commitment of any kind?

SINGER: We need a president, we need politicians, we need sociologists. I don't say we don't need them, but I say once a writer becomes in his writing a sociologist or a politician, he discovers nothing, he only spoils his work. He can, after he has finished writing his novel, go out and make a speech for a particular candidate or for whomever he loves. This will not do any damage. But his novel cannot be a political treatise.

BURGIN: To the extent that you do involve yourself in political matters, what kind of political animal are you?

SINGER: I am actually conservative. I don't believe that by flattering the masses all the time we really achieve much.

BURGIN: I don't agree with you, but neither of us is a political man and in an argument of this nature I don't suppose either of us would change the other's mind.

Let me ask you about the "cultural vulgarity" you once talked to me about in connection with Israel. Are there any specific things that are happening in Israel now or the last time you visited it that strike you as vulgar, and if so, why?

SINGER: Their making fun of Yiddish is a very vulgar trait to me because if Yiddish-speaking Jews had not suffered for hundreds of years in exile, there wouldn't be a Jewish country now. To try to erase hundreds of years of Jewish history in Eastern Europe and to spit on their language is very vulgar. I'm happy to say that in Israel now at least some of the leaders have recognized this themselves. They are trying to turn back, to recognize Yiddish and to realize how important it was. After the Balfour Declaration, when there was a meeting in Israel and they spoke Yiddish, fanatics came in and beat up the audience or they tore up Yiddish books. They did all kinds of brutal things. Thank God, this time is past.

BURGIN: You have acknowledged very strong feelings about Israel's place in history.

SINGER: It never happened in the world that a people were exiled from their country and afterwards did not assimilate. As a rule, when people are exiled or even if they just emigrate, after a generation or two they become assimilated in their new environment. Millions and millions of Germans emigrated to this country; they all became "real" Americans. There is no trace that they were German except perhaps their names. They have forgotten the German language. But the Jewish people have been in exile for two thousand years; they have lived in hundreds of countries, spoken many languages and still kept their old language, Hebrew. They kept their Aramaic, later their Yiddish; they kept their books; they did not forsake their faith; and after two thousand years they are going back to Israel. This is such a special case in human history that if it hadn't happened, no one would believe it possible. If someone had written a story about such people, the critics would have called it a fantasy. This makes the history of the Jewish people unique. This power of being a minority, a persecuted minority, and staying with one's culture for two thousand years denies all sociological and psychological theories about nations or collectives. From this point of view, Zionism is important. It reveals that sometimes collectives can also accomplish the most exceptional things. The Jews are a unique people in the history of humanity; their attachment to their history is baffling. They even stay attached to the length of their exile.

BURGIN: This leads me to the whole question of assimilation. A recurrent theme in your novels and stories deals with Jews who have assimilated as opposed to Jews who haven't. Do you regard yourself as having partially assimilated?

SINGER: No, I don't think I am an assimilated Jew. I still speak Yiddish, the language which my father and mother spoke.

BURGIN: But you moved away from certain tenets in the religion.

SINGER: Well, I'm not as religious as my parents were. From the religious point of view, you can say I'm assimilated, but from a cultural point of view, I'm not. I stay with my people. My Jewishness is not something of which I'm ashamed, but the very opposite. I'm proud of it. I keep accentuating all the time that I am a Jew. I write about Jews. I write in Jewish languages. I began to write in Hebrew.

BURGIN: What is your definition of a Jew who's assimilated?

SINGER: An assimilated Jew is a man who is ashamed of his origin, who denies his roots. He wants to make believe that he's somebody else.

BURGIN: May I take myself as an example? I grew up in a town that was predominately Jewish, but all the Jews that I knew were assimilated.

SINGER: If you were born in an assimilated house, I cannot accuse you. If your father or grandfather was already an assimilationist, there is little you can do to mend this situation unless you are ready to make a great effort.

BURGIN: But what is an assimilationist? My father, for instance, doesn't observe religious practices, but he has never denied his Jewishness; neither would he flaunt it.

SINGER: Did he send you to a Jewish school when you were a boy?

BURGIN: No.

SINGER: Did he teach you Hebrew or Yiddish?

BURGIN: No. But he would not deny that he was Jewish. He was in no way ashamed of being Jewish. When we were in Europe, he wouldn't visit certain regions that had discriminated against Jews.

SINGER: I would say that he was a partial assimilationist, because if he would believe that Jewishness is important, why not teach it to his child? Take, for example, my son. My son is now a Hebrew journalist; he lives in Israel, he belongs to a kibbutz. I did not want him to say, "I happen to be a Jew but it means nothing to me." These people can be great scholars and whatever else they might be, but they can never be great writers.

BURGIN: Why is that so? That needs to be backed up.

SINGER: Because literature is completely connected with one's origin, with one's roots. The great masters were all rooted in their people. Tolstoy, Dostoyevsky, and Gogol were as Russian, as Ukrainian as they could be. Dostoyevsky even became a Pan-Slavist. He wanted the whole world to become Russian. The only real writer who had no roots was Kafka. I would say about

Kafka that he was looking for his roots. He tried to get them. But when you take a man like Koestler, who preaches assimilation and tries so hard to show that the Jews are not even Jews, he fails both as a man of dignity and as a writer. A Jewish writer who denies his Jewishness is neither a Jew nor does he really belong to any other group.

BURGIN: If you had fallen in love with a non-Jewish woman, could you possibly have married her?

SINGER: I don't know. Sometimes love is stronger than a man's convictions. My wife comes from an assimilated house . . . she was born in Germany and her father was assimilated. Their Jewishness was only for Rosh Hashanah and Yom Kippur. When we got acquainted, I told her that I'm a Yiddish writer. This looked strange to her. "What does it mean, a Yiddish writer? What kind of a career can a Yiddish writer make? What is the sense of writing in a language which is dying and for people who are backward?" But I felt that Yiddish and the Jewish people and their language were important for me and that if I wanted to be a real writer I would have to write about them and not about the American Gentiles of whom I knew nothing. I had to remember my youth and to stay with my language and with the people I knew best. An assimilated writer never does this. He tries always to go into a group where he does not completely belong.

BURGIN: You often speak with a kind of disdain about the assimilated Jew. What is so bad about him? I mean as a human being, not as a writer.

SINGER: In one sense he is the salt of humanity with his tremendous energy and ambition. But being salt, he gives humanity high blood pressure. He's neither a real Jew nor a real Gentile. He has no roots in any group. He digs all the time in other people's soil, but he never reaches any roots. He tries consciously and subconsciously to wipe out the individuality of nations and cultures. Like those who built the Tower of Babel, he tries to transmute the whole world into one style. He often preaches a sort of liberalism which is false and is the opposite of liberal. The worst thing about the assimilationist is that he has no pride. He always wants to be where he is not wanted.

BURGIN: Sometimes your characters from different religious traditions are able to love each other. For example, in *The Slave* with Jacob and Sarah.

SINGER: Yes, I don't say that you cannot love people from another nation, but Jacob remained what he was. Of course, he tried to assimilate Sarah, but he succeeded only partially. She, too, could not forget *her* roots, no matter how much she tried to get roots in Jewish life. For her it was not enough that she loved him; she made an effort to acquire new roots.

BURGIN: But she did that for him.

SINGER: Yes, but it does not matter; it's not important how you get your roots. You can, in some cases, change your roots. But for a writer this may be fatal. His art is the first victim of such arbitrary changes.

BURGIN: Your ideas almost make me feel doomed, because although I'm a fiction writer, I'm the product of what they call a mixed marriage. I think I told you this.

SINGER: You have to find your roots.

BURGIN: Which are half and half.

SINGER: Write about the people you know best, whether they are Jews or Protestants or Turks. If you write about the things and the people you know best, you discover your roots, even if they are new roots, partial roots. In other words, you should not deny your father's roots or your mother's roots.

BURGIN: I was raised by my father to be a freethinker with a cosmopolitan and very liberal point of view.

SINGER: I don't think a Marxist has ever written a great book of fiction. This is because a writer must have roots and Marxism is against roots. A Marxist is a cosmopolitan or tries to be one, while a real writer belongs to his people, to his environment, whether he likes it or not. The cosmopolitan never writes anything unique. He is a generalizer. You can say of Gogol that he was politically naïve or that he was a reactionary, but he stuck to his Ukrainian roots. The idea of roots is not to deny anything. You have to make the best of your origin and upbringing. You did not grow up in a vacuum. Your case, Mr. Burgin, is a case of complicated roots, mixed roots, but roots they are. If you are going to write a cosmopolitan novel, just about a human being, you will never succeed, because there isn't such a thing as "just a human being."

BURGIN: Meaning what?

SINGER: You cannot write a love story of two human beings without dealing with their background—what nation they belonged to, what language their fathers spoke at home, and where they grew up. When you talk about a writer you always mention his nation, his language. Writers, more than any other artists, belong to their nation, their language, their history, their culture. They are both highly individualistic and highly attached to their origin.

BURGIN: Why is everybody so obsessed with their religion, with their country? Why must this be such an overriding issue?

SINGER: Because of the differences. The difference between an Irishman and an Italian may mean little if they both are engineers, but if they write novels, this difference is of the highest importance. Sean O'Casey will not write like Pirandello. He's Irish and being Irish is his literary fate. When you want to write a letter, let's say to someone who lives in Poland, you cannot address it to just "a man." It will never arrive, because there are three or four billion *men* in the world. You have to address it to Mr. So-and-So, give the name of the country, the city, the street, the number of the house, and sometimes the number of the apartment. The same thing is true in literature. Of course, we know that you are writing about a man, but the question is *what* man, where does he come from, where does he live, what language does he speak? You have to give his spiritual address. Of course, an address in literature is different from an address on an envelope, but the idea is the same. Go from the general to the particular, until we know there is only one such person. Literature assumes that no men or women are completely alike. Individuality is the axiom of literature. The ability to convey individuality and to make it interesting is the very essence of talent. The protagonists of bad fiction works are made of cardboard. I must add that wars and revolutions destroy not only people but precious cultural roots while peace creates them and nourishes them.

7.

Literary inflation . . . The genesis of stories . . . When we sleep, we all become geniuses . . . Conditions for writing . . . Taking models from life . . . Experts at fingerprints

BURGIN: You often mention the need for suspense in literature. Why is suspense so important?

SINGER: Man, more than all other animals, suffers from boredom. Sometimes I think man's boredom begins in the womb. More people die from boredom than we ever realize. Art should reduce human boredom, not make it worse (as is often the case with talentless writers and critics). The politicians have one basic remedy for boredom and this is war or revolution. Art should create a less dangerous suspense. There is no excuse for literature which does not entertain the reader, or does not help the reader escape from the tedium of life.

BURGIN: Do you really believe that literature still possesses untapped resources of entertainment?

SINGER: The masters of the nineteenth century were all great entertainers in the highest sense of the word. Poetry—especially with its brevity and its rhyme and rhythm—was a source of delight to the reader for many generations. We are witnessing the demise of poetry as a means of entertaining the reader and lifting up his spirit. Modernistic poetry does not speak to any reader, does not stir his or her emotions. It seems to be written for the professors of literature, so that they can write explanations and commentaries about its pseudo-profundity. The reader does not understand it, does not enjoy it. There is the danger that the novel and the drama might go in the same direction—becoming so utterly esoteric as to become completely useless.

BURGIN: Since you've just mentioned "explanations and commentaries," I wonder what your definition is of good and bad criticism.

SINGER: Hippolyte Taine has written ten volumes to prove that the artist is a product of his time and his environment. His disciples have said the same thing in thousands of volumes. But it is a lie just the same. Art and talent are not as much a product of their time as of the genes. Talent is born. Even the talent to recognize what is good and bad in art is born, and comes from the genes. Just as some people are born deaf to music so are some people born deaf to the values of literature. No doctor or professor can help them. Taste or lack of taste is basically biological.

BURGIN: You once said in an interview that we are suffering from a literary inflation. What exactly do you mean by this?

SINGER: Many words have been misused to such a degree they have lost all meaning and all value. They express neither any spiritual nor any emotional qualities. Because of this, it has become more and more difficult for a writer to be precise. He has to exaggerate to be understood. No words have suffered as much from literary inflation as those which express emotions. While the vocabulary of nouns and verbs has grown, the words which express emotions have remained almost status quo. As to the words which were created by modern psychology, they have been precarious from the very beginning—and they cannot be used in any serious literary description, except perhaps in quotation marks. The writer who tries to be precise is forced to reject almost all adjectives. He has to function practically with only those nouns which express clear and simple images. The language of technology does not stir the reader's emotions; it has neither the power to entertain the reader nor to lift his spirit. It may sound like a paradox, but the thicker the dictionaries become, the poorer the language is becoming for the writer of fiction. The art of writing nowadays lies not in finding new words, but in avoiding more and more those words which have become nothing but empty clichés, like "good, bad, decent, immoral, charming, ugly, noble, clever, attractive," and many, many others which are now stale.

BURGIN: Doesn't this sound hopeless to you?

SINGER: I sometimes think that we will have to borrow image words from the Chinese. To be serious, the talented writer will have to learn how to express himself in a vocabulary which will become poorer in time instead of richer. I guess that Joyce must have felt the danger of language dying from anemia. However, I don't believe that he found the real remedy.

BURGIN: How about Yiddish?

SINGER: The Yiddish language has been used less than French, German, Spanish, English, and other such popular languages. It still contains quite a number of adjectives and idioms which don't reek of banality. This may be true of a number of other languages which were not used and misused by many millions of people. The trouble is that idioms—no matter how charming and meaningful—are only valid when the writer uses dialogue. When he speaks himself he must avoid idioms and try to be as precise as possible in his prose. Since dramatic works are all dialogue, the playwright is free to use more idioms than any other writer. The problem is that idioms cannot really be translated into other languages. They are more national, more clannish, more attached to the roots of the group than other linguistic media. They are born and die in their environment.

BURGIN: Can you tell me more about what is special in the Yiddish language as far as literature is concerned?

SINGER: The Yiddish-speaking writer actually uses three languages: Old German, Hebrew, and Aramaic. He also has linguistic roots in the Slavic languages. While Yiddish did not develop a rich scientific and technological vocabulary, it has excelled in creating words which describe character and personality. It was Freudian before Freud. It has told many things about our subconscious in its own primitive fashion. It is a language with a sense of humor, if one may say so, and is not easily translatable.

BURGIN: Borges said that he could envision a world without novels—but not without tales, stories, or verses. What are your feelings about that remark?

SINGER: I feel that once we have novels we will never be without them. Once man has created something, he will come back to it. There may be some periods of history with shorter novels or longer novels, or there may be novels which might deal with topics other than love, although it's hard for me to imagine this. There is, however, no reason why the novel should disappear, or television, or radio. Everything which man has invented has a chance to stay, one way or another.

BURGIN: So you don't feel, as Borges seemed to, that the story and the poem are somehow eternal literary forms and superior to the novel?

SINGER: The novel *is* a story, it *is* a tale. It is only a larger story. Because it is large, you can put in stories within the story. If the novel has no story, it's no novel.

BURGIN: You once told me you felt you had a greater command of the short story.

SINGER: A short story is a lot easier to plan and it can be more accomplished than a novel. If you have a short story to tell, you can work on it so that from your point of view you have made it perfect. But a novel, especially a large novel, can never be perfect even in the eyes of the creator—if the creator is a person capable of self-criticism. The chance of having flaws becomes larger proportionally to the length of the novel. A longer novel has more flaws than a short novel—except if the longer novel is written by a master and the shorter one by a bungler. Tolstoy's *The Death of Ivan Ilyich* has fewer flaws than *War and Peace*.

BURGIN: I remember Faulkner commenting while describing the genesis of *The Sound and the Fury* that he couldn't get an image out of his mind: a girl climbing a tree and getting her underpants dirty from the bark, and from that image he found his starting point. How does it work with you? Do you proceed differently when you are writing your fiction?

SINGER: I am always looking for the story, but in the beginning there's a kind of atmosphere which precedes the story. When I wrote *Satan in Goray,* the atmosphere was Jewish psychic events—the demons and all those things which make up the atmosphere of *Satan in Goray.* And then I looked for a story to fit the atmosphere. Take, for example, Strindberg's *The Father.* Strindberg's first idea, probably, was that the whole system of fatherhood is false. No father knows for sure that he is the father of his children. This was a most disturbing emotion for Strindberg. And then, out of this emotion, he created his play. Sometimes the story comes first and the ideas and emotions come later. Sometimes the story itself is the idea. Actually, in our brain ideas, emotions, and images come together. All these divisions are seldom real.

BURGIN: But what about Isaac Bashevis Singer? How does your work come to you? I imagine different stories come in different ways.

SINGER: For me, it's a desire to record either emotions or a system of emotions or an environment which I think no one has ever described before. With *The Family Moskat* I said to myself, "Warsaw has just been destroyed. No one will ever see the Warsaw I knew. Let me write about it. Let this Warsaw not disappear forever." Just like Homer (forgive me the comparison), who was the greatest of them all, felt about Troy, I felt about Warsaw in my own small way. But I said to myself, "I can only write about the Jewish Warsaw, not the Catholic Warsaw." I didn't know the Catholics as well as the Jews.

BURGIN: Then how did the *story* come to you?

SINGER: This story of *The Family Moskat* didn't come at once. I knew a man like Meshulam Moskat would be interesting to write about, but I needed a story to tell. And then, I said to myself, if there must be a story it has to be a love story, because I already knew then that you cannot really write a novel without a love story. Many writers have tried and they always failed.

I also wanted to have someone who's kind of similar to me, like this Asa Heshel, although he's not actually me. And then I knew that Asa Heshel alone would not make the novel interesting. There must be other people. I would say it's the process of creating a world of emotions. Then you must slowly develop the story. The story and its tension—in connection with genuine characters—is the most difficult thing to develop in a novel.

BURGIN: Are there any cases where you envision your stories quickly?

SINGER: There are cases where short stories come quickly. Even today I had an idea for a story. It came in a second.

BURGIN: Do dreams ever influence what you write?

SINGER: I don't know if they do, but I always dream.

BURGIN: Many people feel writing and dreaming are closely related.

SINGER: When we sleep, we all become geniuses in a way, because only there do we see things that are so unusual and mysterious and at the same time see them with such strong emotion.

BURGIN: Everything is condensed and seems to resonate with meaning.

SINGER: There is an expression in Hebrew, "the maker of dreams." It seems the maker of dreams is the greatest genius of all time. He's everything; a mystic and a symbolist and even a profound realist. However, most people cannot dream when they are awake. They only dream at night and later they forget their dreams. But the artist dreams while he is awake. The making of art is a way of dreaming. The only difference is that what a dream can do in two minutes, it sometimes takes an artist years to do. What the purpose of the dream is, I don't know. I have a feeling that the dream is a kind of built-in entertainment in man. Since in olden times men couldn't have gone to the theater or to see movies, dreams gave him the minimum of entertainment which he needed or he would have died from boredom altogether. But there is more to it than entertainment. Just as a talented writer writes books to entertain people but gives them more than entertainment, the same thing is true with a dream.

BURGIN: Are you familiar with Freud's *Interpretation of Dreams?* Does it mean anything to you?

SINGER: I would say the dream has more to it than what Freud finds in it. Whatever definition you make about the dream, you limit it. Language is such that whatever you say, you create a limitation instead of giving the full meaning.

BURGIN: The merging of dreams with waking life is also a recurrent theme of yours. I'm thinking now of the dissolution of reality that we find in one of my favorite stories of yours: "The Dance"—you remember it, of course.

SINGER: This little story? Yes, yes. It was published in a magazine called *Nimrod.*

BURGIN: I think that magazine still exists.

SINGER: Yes, because I just published another story there. It's a little magazine published by the University of Tulsa.

BURGIN: When did you publish it? How long ago?

SINGER: "The Dance" must have been published about eight or nine years ago. I'm happy that you like it.

BURGIN: I'm curious how you regard your "canon of fictions," whether you have any favorite stories or novels.

SINGER: I don't have favorites. It is like a father who has ten children and he likes them all, and if you say you love one child most, he will agree with you because he loves it, too, but he will not agree that it's better than the others.

BURGIN: So you don't think you've succeeded in achieving your aims more in certain stories and novels than in others?

SINGER: I feel that I succeeded more or less in all of them as much as I could. Of course, if I would have worked more, if I would have had time to rewrite them, I might have made them better, but taking into consideration the time which I was ready to give them, I feel that I did more or less, as they say, my best.

BURGIN: And you don't feel that some are stronger than others?

SINGER: I think that this is absolutely left to the reader, to the critic to decide.

BURGIN: Don't you criticize your works for yourself?

SINGER: No, not this way. I never think about what is better and what is worse.

BURGIN: Maybe not in such crude terms, but don't you ever in retrospect think, "No, this isn't at a level that I'm really capable of"?

SINGER: I don't reread them. I know that there are faults in the larger novels, in *The Family Moskat* and in *The Manor,* maybe more faults than in *The Slave* and in *The Magician of Lublin* and maybe not. I don't know.

BURGIN: Getting back to your method of working— you said once that you don't really invent characters.

SINGER: I always take models from life. Most of the models from *Satan in Goray* are from the town of Bilgoray, where my grandfather was a Rabbi. Near Bilgoray there is a village called Goray, and the people of Bilgoray are so like the people of Goray that I could easily see them in Goray. Actually, in some cases I even took the real names of the people, like Mordecai Joseph. When I write I use living characters.

BURGIN: Do you have any "rules" for writing good prose?

SINGER: I have a number of rules for myself. One of them is that when you write a novel or a novella, make each chapter tell a new development of the story and contain as much information as the first one. It must be revealing, rich in images, in character description, small in quantity and large in quality.

BURGIN: What are your "rules" when you write short stories?

SINGER: It must be short. A number of writers make their short stories unusually long. Chekhov and Maupassant never did this. Their short stories were really *short.* Of course, it should have suspense from beginning to end. With bad writers the suspense begins to diminish almost immediately and then evaporates altogether. As for the process itself, first I get the idea or the emotion. Then I need a plot, a story with a beginning, a middle, and an end, just as Aristotle said it should be. A story to me must have some surprise. The plot should be such that when you read the first page, you don't know what the second will be. When you read the second page, you don't know what the third will be, because this is how life is, full of little surprises. The second condition is that I must have a passion to write the story. Sometimes I have a very good plot, but somehow the passion to write this story is missing. If this is the case, I would not write it.

And the third condition is the most important. I must be convinced, or at least have the illusion, that I am the only one who could write this particular story or this particular novel. Let's take, for example, "Gimpel the Fool." Another writer can write a hundred better stories, but the story of Gimpel the Fool, the way I tell it, is a story which only I could have written—not my colleagues or, say, writers who were brought up in English.

Now, for a plot you need characters. So instead of inventing characters, I contemplate the people whom I have met in my life who would fit into this story. I sometimes combine two characters and from them make one. I may take a person whom I met in this country and put him in Poland or vice versa. But just the same, I must have a model.

All real painters painted from models. They knew that Nature has more surprises than our imagination can ever invent. When you take a model, a character whom you know, you already attach yourself to Nature and all its surprises, idiosyncrasies, and peculiarities.

I don't invent characters because the Almighty has already invented millions and billions of them. Humanity may become a million years old and I'm sure that in all this time there will not be two people who are really alike. Experts at fingerprints do not create fingerprints. They learn how to read them. In the same way the writer reads human characters.

BURGIN: You said once that sometimes you develop the character to such an extent that the model becomes almost lost.

SINGER: Yes, I almost forget the model. In the beginning I'm always looking at the model, but after I have developed the character more and more, the picture becomes richer than the model and then I can afford to forget it. But even this isn't really so good. It's better never to let the model go.

You'll see that real painters often have models. They look and they paint. And sometimes you ask yourself, "Why do they have to look at this person a million times? They have already seen his face." But that isn't true. Every time the artist looks up he sees something else, some new variation. This is very important. I think it's a tragedy that literature stopped looking at models. Some writers are so interested in "isms," in ideologies and in theories, that they think that the model cannot

80

add much. But actually all the theories and all the ideas become stale in no time, while what Nature delivers to us is never stale. What Nature creates has an element of eternity in it.

8.

Betrayal and free will . . . Error is only a
human conception . . . Schopenhauer and
the Cabalists . . . A millionaire in emotions
. . . The universal novel

BURGIN: I'm interested in discussing various themes I
find recurring in your works. One is the theme of betrayal—men betray women, women betray men, children betray parents, people betray their religions or
betray God.

SINGER: What bothers me more than anything else is
that men betray themselves. For example, a man makes
a decision to be a good socialist and then he becomes a
phony socialist, a Stalinist. This is very much connected
with free will—because if man would really apply his
free will, he could make a decision and do as he decides.
I would say a great part of human history is a history of
self-betrayal and betrayal of others. These things are
very connected. Would you like to talk more about
them?

BURGIN: Yes.

SINGER: The Jews, according to the Torah, accepted
the Torah at Mount Sinai, but according to the story of

the Bible, they never really kept the Torah. When you read the Book of Samuel, and Kings, you see that most of our kings did not keep the Torah. The story of almost every king ends with the words "and he didn't do what was right in the eyes of God." He served idols, he didn't get rid of the harlots, he sacrificed to false gods, he cultivated false prophets, and so on. When we come to the story of Christianity, we all know that while Jesus preached love and so did his disciples or apostles, Christianity still had many people who betrayed the New Testament, who preached the Sermon on the Mount and did the very opposite. They hated, they made inquisitions, they persecuted minorities, all in the name of love. People who proclaimed love and brotherhood and equality betrayed themselves immediately after they came to power.

Some writers also betray themselves. They decide at first to write not for money but to express what they honestly believe. After a while, they abandon their principles and resort to all kinds of maneuvers—gaining friends, organizing cliques, and so on, praising mediocrity and attacking real talent—all this to feather their own nest.

BURGIN: Another of your recurring themes or motifs is the idea of a random element in life, of errors.

Sometimes it seems as if these "errors" you describe in your fiction are self-willed. For example, Yasha's attempted robbery in *The Magician of Lublin*.

SINGER: According to Spinoza, there are no errors in the universe, errors are only errors from the human point of view. You would never say, for example, that an animal committed an error. Error is only a human conception. We would certainly never say that a stone commits an error when it falls on a roof. Because we assume that a person has free will, we say that he has made a mistake. The truth is that the belief in free will is a categorical imperative. We cannot live without believing in it. You can say a hundred times it does not exist, just as you can say gravity does not exist. But while you say gravity does not exist, you are still walking on the earth, you don't fly up to the sky. The very fact that we all talk about human errors is proof that we believe in man's free will.

BURGIN: In relation to the notion of free will, you refer a number of times in your writings and conversation to Schopenhauer, who believed in a blind will motivating Nature. If I'm not mistaken, Schopenhauer equated genius with "objectivity," or the ability to remove oneself from the will.

SINGER: Schopenhauer is full of contradictions, but just the same he is wonderful. He is a genius. I don't agree with Schopenhauer that the will is blind. I could agree with him that the thing-in-itself is will, but I don't agree with him for a moment that a blind power could create an amoeba, a flower, or a man. What I admire in Schopenhauer is his courage to be a pessimist. Most of the philosophers tried one way or another to paint a beautiful universe and to give people hopes which were nothing more than wishful thinking. Schopenhauer had the courage to say that we are living in a world of evil. In this respect, he resembles the Cabalists. They, too, call this world a den of demons, the lowest of all the worlds. The only difference is: the Cabalists say that this world is the weakest link in God's chain, unless we make an effort to live rightly. The Cabalists believed in free will when they said that if human beings behave well, then they keep the chain of creation in order. But Schopenhauer never went in this direction. According to the Cabalists, God has compensated man for creating him in the lowest of all worlds by giving him free will. Schopenhauer is a fatalist. Just the same, he maintains that intellect can light up blind will, mitigate it, even make it reverse itself. This seems a casuistic compromise, but it contains deep insight into the human condition.

What I also like in Schopenhauer is that he was a beautiful writer, a sharp observer of human affairs. He was a great psychologist. As far as psychology is concerned, he really investigated human life—he had a great knowledge of human passions. Those who believe in Hegel hate Schopenhauer, just as Hegel himself would have hated Schopenhauer if he knew him. Schopenhauer despised Hegel because Hegel gave false hopes to humanity. His *Zeitgeist* was nothing but an idol, a phrase, a belief that kings and politicians can correct all evils. And let's not forget that on the soil of Hegel, Marx grew. Schopenhauer had no disciples, except maybe one, Hartmann, who is a chapter in himself.

BURGIN: I notice that word came up again—passions—which is the name of a recent collection of your stories. It could be an appropriate title for any of your books. In your work it seems to have at least two sides to it: one is that people are victims of their passions and it makes for a perilous world, but it's also equally perilous to be without them.

SINGER: I have always felt that God was very frugal, very stingy in bestowing gifts on us. He didn't give us enough intellect, enough physical strength, but when He came to emotions, to passions, He was very lavish. He gave us so many emotions and such strong ones that every human being, even if he is an idiot, is a millionaire in emotions. Sometimes we ask: Why do we need so many emotions which make us suffer and confuse us? When I observe animals, I see that their emotions are quite limited. The emotions of horses or of elephants are more or less the equivalent of their behavior. You will never say about an animal that its emotions drove it in one direction while it acted in another. An animal acts perfectly according to its feelings, while man cannot exist if he gives in to all his feelings. Not only would he break the Commandments, he would break his neck. When you drive a motorcycle, or a car, you sometimes have the desire to reach the maximum speed. However, you know that if you use too much gasoline you may be punished or the car may be broken or you may kill somebody. The more man progresses, the more he has to curb his passions. In this respect, he is a complete exception in the creation of life. All the other living things we know do not curb their passions. A man can sometimes teach an animal to curb its emotions by rewarding it or punishing it with some food. The animal is learning but this is not free will.

I would say that the very essence of literature is the war between emotion and intellect, between life and death. Because if you use all of your emotions indiscriminately, you will kill yourself. Although the man who commits suicide is often a man of intellect, he seldom kills himself because of the conviction that it is better not to be than to be. In most cases, it's from anger or a desire to punish somebody or to escape from himself. So emotions are the very topic of literature. Actually, all the arts deal with emotions. When you take away the emotions from a mathematician, he may still be able to make his calculations, but when literature becomes too intellectual, which means it begins to ignore the emotions and becomes brainy and cold, it loses everything.

BURGIN: I take it that you wouldn't subscribe to the beliefs of, say, Nietzsche or Freud in a single central passion or drive that essentially dominates human behavior.

SINGER: I agree with Spinoza where he says that everything can become a passion. It means actually that there is nothing in life which cannot become a passion. The man who collects stamps can become so passionate about them that he would endanger his life to get some silly stamp from some faraway country. The number of passions is almost as large as the number of objects or the number of notions. Of course, there are the main passions like sex and power. But all the other things can also evoke passions, even great passions.

BURGIN: Borges once said that a writer really has only three or four stories or passions to impart and that everything he writes is a variation on these few themes.

SINGER: A good writer writes about things that stir *his* passions and each man has only a limited number of them.

BURGIN: Is that true of you, too?

SINGER: Yes. I don't have thousands of great passions. But a writer can describe countless variations on every one. When you read Tolstoy, you see him and his passions, too, in everything he writes. Take *War and Peace* and *Anna Karenina*. Here is Pierre and there is Levin and they are both the same type of person. They are both like Tolstoy more or less, or as Tolstoy might have been in their situations. These people who complain that the writer repeats himself are not really just, because if he hadn't repeated himself, he wouldn't have been true to his basic desires.

Every writer must write on his own topics, which are connected with his main passions, with the things he is pondering about, or brooding over. This is in part what gives a writer his charm and makes him genuine. It's only the amateur who will take any topic. He will go somewhere, he will hear a story—something, anything —and immediately it will become "his story." The real writer writes only stories which are connected with his personality, with his character, with his way of seeing the world. So in a way when we read the books of the great writers—when we read, let's say, *The Brothers Karamazov*—we have the typical déjà vu feeling. Nevertheless, because Dostoyevsky is a great writer, we want to see him do it again in some different way.

BURGIN: On one level, your work as a whole constitutes an imaginative partial reconstruction of the history of the Jews, the Polish-Yiddish-speaking Jews. Did you intend, like Balzac or Proust or Faulkner, that your fiction would form a kind of grand design?

SINGER: I never intended to write the so-called human comedy. Fiction can be very grand if you stay in your element with your own passions and your own opinions. But if you go out and try to make it a coherent philosophy, it never becomes one. After all, what Balzac tells us is about French people, not necessarily about all people. He stays within his own society. He doesn't tell us about the Chinese.

BURGIN: I meant that, within that restriction, was it your intention when you started writing a certain novel to form a connected whole? Did you already foresee that you would write about the Jews of many different generations?

SINGER: I don't think it is good for a writer to sit down and say, "I'm going to write the human comedy, the human tragedy, the paradox of marriage, etc." The best thing for the writer is to write the way he feels at the moment, and later on, if he will have done a lifetime of work, some critic can try to make it into a point of view or a philosophy. The writer should not bother with this. He should write about his own milieu, his own passions, and not try to make his book "the novel which will end all novels," the universal novel after which no one will have anything else to say. This is a silly kind of ambition. Because many, many other talents will live in different generations, will have different points of view and different passions and different milieus. What did Proust do? He described his family and nothing else. To say that his family embodied the whole world is a wild exaggeration. Human life is millions of times richer than what any writer, no matter how great he is, can give us.

9.

Literature and religion . . . A silent God
and the language of deeds . . . Talents are
born . . . Shaw and Tolstoy . . .
"Accidents"

BURGIN: Sartre once said that literature will replace
religion. I wonder how you feel about that comment.

SINGER: My reaction is that literature will never replace religion.

BURGIN: He goes on to say in *Being and Nothingness:*
"The project of the twentieth-century man is to become God," etc.

SINGER: I think it's completely false. Literature hasn't
really done anything for humanity which could be compared to religion, because people *lived* according to
religion, they died for religion. Take the Jewish people.
The very fact that they have existed for thousands of
years in all these terrible circumstances was because
they believed in God, in Providence, and in the hereaf-
ter. What has literature done to be compared to faith?
What have novels done? They entertain people, this is
true. And it's important. People need to be entertained, but no novel, no poem, and no short story can

take the place of the Ten Commandments. So what Sartre said was a wild exaggeration. It also shows how blind some people are about literature, how terribly important it seems to them.

BURGIN: Couldn't one say, however, that the Bible is a form of literature, too?

SINGER: To be a religious person, it's not enough to read the Commandments—you have to *practice* them. Religion becomes literature only when people don't take it seriously anymore. The pious Jews consider the Torah of the highest importance but only as long as the Torah is practiced. If the man is a scholar and he doesn't keep the Commandments, they consider him a heretic and a traitor of Israel.

BURGIN: You characterize novels as primarily "entertainments," yet we know of cases from the past which strike us as probably true—about Dostoyevsky spending nights weeping over the fates of his characters, of Kafka approaching writing as if it were a spiritual activity—and I feel quite certain that you must have experienced similar emotions. Is that mere entertainment, or doesn't that reveal a quality that transcends it?

SINGER: It may be only entertainment, or in some cases a little more than entertainment, but it can never take the place of religion. What did people learn from Dostoyevsky? He hasn't shown humanity how to live. He was great in pondering the eternal questions but he didn't show us any new way. The very essence of religion is not in reading sacred books but in living what is written there. If you read the Bible as just poetry or prose or history, then you are no longer a religious person. I think it's important to talk about it because it is happening in our time that people think that by reading some important book you "become" what the book preaches. It's the same thing as if one would say that reading the books of Karl Marx could take the place of socialism. For a socialist, socialism has to be *made*. He has to fight for it.

BURGIN: You have said to me that morally, ethically, and spiritually, man has made little progress through the centuries.

SINGER: People are progressing technologically but they're not progressing morally. I don't see any moral progress.

BURGIN: You see no progress from any point in history until now? Would you go that far?

SINGER: I really don't know enough history. I don't think anybody knows enough to "judge."

BURGIN: I'm sure you know a good deal more than most people.

SINGER: I know mostly about the Jewish people. I think that in the last two hundred years—from the point of view of Jewishness—we have regressed, not progressed. Anyhow, to me the twentieth century was not the century of any moral or religious growth.

BURGIN: It's often depicted as the century when the Jews reached the height of achievement in the arts and sciences and in general recognition.

SINGER: I speak about religion. We had a number of scientists, prime ministers . . . The Jews have a country now. They are recognized in a number of countries, but attaining worldly assets is not really the aim of Judaism. When Moses gave the Torah, he believed that it's possible to create a nation of spiritual people, a kingdom of priests, and a holy nation. This never became a reality. Moses wasn't allowed to cross the Jordan because what he wanted to create and what actually happened in the years after the revelation on Mount Sinai were two different things altogether.

We have material progress in Israel today, but our greatest achievements were not in Israel actually, but in exile. It's only after the Talmud was composed—between the Talmud and the Emancipation—that the Jews lived a highly religious life. The Bible tells us that our ancestors were idolators most of the time. Our kings, with a few exceptions, did not do what was right in the eyes of Jehovah. So when you say there was progress, the question is, progress in what? Technologically, we have progress . . . we didn't have television or jet planes. Morally, I don't see any progress in this century.

BURGIN: You once said to me, "I'm disgusted with the way things are with life in general . . ." Yet you have stated many times that you believe in God.

SINGER: I believe in God.

BURGIN: How do you reconcile for yourself this world where man makes no progress . . . where ethically and spiritually man has not progressed . . . with such an unwavering belief in God? Is it something inculcated in you from childhood?

SINGER: I believe in God but I have my doubts about revelation. I would say that I have no proof whatsoever that God reveals Himself or tells us how to behave, what He wants. I believe that God is a silent God, and He must have a very good reason why He is silent. If He would begin to talk, He would have to speak in three thousand languages and in all kinds of dialects. God speaks in deeds, but the language of deeds is so large—its vocabulary is as large as the universe perhaps. So we only understand a very small part of His language. Everything man says about God is pure guesswork. But since I believe in God's existence and since God created man and formed his brain, I believe also that there must be something of the divine in men's ideas about Him—even if they are far from being adequate.

BURGIN: What do you understand of His language?

SINGER: I understand it the way a child of three years who can use a few words—"Papa, Mama, bread"—understands when he hears adults discuss higher matters. Because the language of deeds is so large and our understanding of it is so small, I would say that God has revealed Himself in very, very small doses. He is a hidden God. But just the same, I feel that He's there.

BURGIN: Were there any instances in your life that confirmed this belief?

SINGER: I cannot believe in what the materialists say—that the universe is a result of some explosion which took place billions of years ago. If you don't believe that the universe is an accident, you have to believe that there was some plan in its becoming—some design or some intelligence. And if you believe this, you already believe in God. If you want to insist on calling Him nature, you can call Him nature. But to me, nature is not blind. As a rule, when we say nature, we mean blind nature—a nature which does things according to physical laws only, by sheer causality, without any idea or purpose. Since I don't believe this, I believe in God. You can call Him the absolute—it doesn't make any difference. The word "God" is just as good as any other word.

BURGIN: Do you envision Him in any form or not?

SINGER: I'm inclined to believe that God and the world are identical. God is everything: all spirit, all matter, what is, what was, and what will be, as Spinoza conceived Him. However, according to Spinoza, the Substance, with its infinite number of attributes, has no will, no purpose. I don't believe in this part of Spinoza. I think that we can just as well ascribe to the Substance will and designs and purposes. According to Spinoza, God has two attributes that are known to us—extension and thought. I believe we can ascribe to Him many more—even mercy—although we may not see it. Here is the place where definition and logic end and faith begins. Pantheism isn't geometry. Without faith it dissolves into nothing.

BURGIN: If I might return to the theme of progress in technology and literature and what it means to you—

you've commented that no matter how great an innovator a writer is, he can never affect life the way scientists affect it.

SINGER: Of course not. In the last, let's say, three hundred years, consider what science has done! It's reversed everything, our whole picture of the material universe. Three hundred years ago, we didn't know about microbes, we didn't know anything about the chemical elements, the electromagnetic phenomena. In three hundred years colossal changes have taken place in science and technology. Newton alone has revolutionized science.

BURGIN: You don't feel there's been a vast change in the content, style, and form of literature in three hundred years? After all, even language has changed.

SINGER: Yes, language has changed, but if you read Homer today, it's still a masterpiece. It is not obsolete. But from the science of the ancient Greeks—except for Euclid—little is still valid. The best literature was written in the nineteenth century as far as the novel and the short story are concerned, but there was a Cervantes before and there were other great prose writers. Literature either tells a story or expresses emotion. There is no major advance in this field. Our knowledge has gone forward with giant steps and still does, but our emotions are the same and so basically is literature. It is not a science but an art. Some professors and critics would like to make a science of it, but they will never succeed.

BURGIN: They look at literature evolutionarily, like a Great Chain of Being.

SINGER: You don't read literature because you want to learn psychology or sociology or any other "ology." Art was made for enjoyment from the very beginning and it will always be so. Of course, to entertain higher spirits you have to be a higher kind of entertainer. But just the same, if it stops entertaining, if it only tries to reveal some truths, it doesn't serve its purpose. Neither does it really reveal any general truth. To me, Joyce's *Ulysses* is almost boring. I don't enjoy this kind of abstruse writing where style is dominant and the story only serves as a container of the style, a frame.

BURGIN: I take it you'd feel the same about Faulkner. *The Sound and the Fury* doesn't move you?

SINGER: I haven't read that book. But when I read a work of fiction and it bores me, I don't care what other qualities it may possess. I don't study literature, I read it for enjoyment.

BURGIN: Do you feel the same way about Beckett?

SINGER: I feel the same way about Beckett. If I would study geometry, I wouldn't look for entertainment. If I want to know how many right angles a triangle has, the theorem has a purpose beyond pleasure. Such a book doesn't have to have beauty, it doesn't have to have any aesthetic construction. If it has beauty, it's an additional good quality but it is not the most important quality. No one can say that Bergson is a greater philosopher than Kant because Bergson had a better style. The question is, what is he saying?

BURGIN: Would you align philosophers more with science than with literature?

SINGER: The truth is that philosophy is neither. It is a discipline and a lore in itself; it is the history of man's endeavor to overreach his capacities.

BURGIN: Certainly Nietzsche is more of a writer than a scientist.

SINGER: Nietzsche is not really a philosopher. The philosophers are people like Spinoza and Kant and Hume and Locke. They didn't have to be interesting, although Hume is. They had to say something and whether what they said has charm or not is not of major importance. The criterion is whether what they said discovered something about God's greatness or man's limitations.

BURGIN: Since so many books have already been written, even more entertaining ones than we can ever read in a lifetime, why should we continue to practice literature?

SINGER: If you have already seen a play, you don't want to see it again. Or if you have read a book once, you seldom want to read it again. So we need new writers. Also, time creates new situations, new complications, new notions.

BURGIN: Don't you think that in the process of being entertained the reader can get some insights into the world around him?

SINGER: We get insights, but no novel teaches you enough psychology for you to become a psychologist. It doesn't teach you enough sociology to become a sociologist. The Communists have decided that all the novels that appear in Soviet Russia have to teach you Leninism. Actually, they don't teach you anything, except the fact that forced writing can never be good.

BURGIN: In commenting on the contemporary literary situation, you talked about "big people" and "little people," and you defined big people as the minority who have a true sensibility. Could you explain why, in your view, so many people with little talent generally control the literary business?

SINGER: Because they and their readers are the majority.

BURGIN: And how did they get to be that way?

SINGER: They were born that way. Talents are *born*. I don't believe that talent really can be made, that society makes them or that circumstances do. The genes don't produce many talents. Talent has been rare in all generations. It is almost a freak of nature. In the one city of New York we now have two hundred publishers and every year they have to publish a number of novels to stay in business. Where can you get so many talents? The number of readers is increasing because literacy is improved. You can teach people how to read, but you can't teach people how to write. So the demand is becoming larger from generation to generation while the supply of the real stuff is still small. The publishers have to call a non-talent a talent to be able to sell a book, because if they waited only for the few people who really understand who's a talent and who's not, they would go out of business. And even if the publishers and critics understand what is what, where do you get the talents? We know, for example, that there were a number of talents in the nineteenth century, which was a blessed century, but even then you could count them on the fingers of one hand or two hands or three hands. In this generation we have for the first time scores of millions of readers and the majority of them read kitsch.

BURGIN: Why does it so often take so long for genuine talents to be recognized?

SINGER: Because if so many non-talents are called talents, the readers and even the critics no longer know who is a talent. Also, small people are big liars. They lie brazenly if they need to, or if they feel like it. The time of idolatry is still here. They call a piece of clay God and force this belief on others with all kinds of tricks. Even in the nineteenth century, real talents were persecuted and non-talents were admired. They persecuted Byron, they persecuted Wilde and many others. A genius like Edgar Allan Poe died in poverty.

BURGIN: Yet Tolstoy and Dostoyevsky were certainly revered in their lifetimes.

SINGER: No, Dostoyevsky was not. Do you know that Dostoyevsky's editor, Katkov, considered him a sixth-rate writer? Dostoyevsky never made a living.

BURGIN: I understood that towards the end of his life . . .

SINGER: He never made a living till the end of his life. It wasn't until maybe fifty or sixty or seventy years later that people began to rediscover him.

BURGIN: Speaking of literary politics, you mentioned a charming anecdote about Tolstoy and George Bernard Shaw; how Tolstoy had to affect an admiration for Shaw . . .

SINGER: Shaw sent Tolstoy his books and Tolstoy wrote him a letter which was a hymn of praise. At the same time he wrote in his diary that he read Shaw and considered him mediocre. Tolstoy felt that he himself belonged to a small minority, and there was always the danger that the would-be talents would attack him. A unique talent like Tolstoy cannot go through life in peace, but must smuggle himself through life with a fear of being utterly misunderstood, even annihilated.

BURGIN: Do you feel that way about yourself?

SINGER: I don't feel so about myself. I don't compare myself to Tolstoy. But I feel that this was true about many important talents of all generations. They felt that non-recognition is actually the law of events here.

BURGIN: I notice in your own career that books like *The Manor, The Estate,* even *The Magician of Lublin* have a quality of nineteenth-century novels. Then there are other works—among which I'd include *A Crown of Feathers, Passions,* and *Enemies, A Love Story*

—in which you seem to take a new direction, not only thematically but in the form itself. There seems to be much more of a contemporary element in those books. Has there been any evolution or change of direction in your lifework?

SINGER: In those collections you will find stories which I wrote twenty years ago, you will find stories which I wrote twenty months ago. There's no chronological order. I would have to go back and find out when they were written, but I feel that some of the stories which I write today are similar to those which I wrote twenty years ago and vice versa. The only evolution I have made is that since I've lived in America over forty years, I've learned something about a new environment. A story about New York cannot be like a story about Bilgoray. It's different, but as far as style is concerned, I think that they are basically the same.

I don't think that literature has made any discoveries, and those which were supposed to have been made are not really discoveries, since some of them made literature regress instead of progress. When it comes to the building of trains or planes, for instance, no one builds them in the way they did in 1904 or 1906. Since they've learned to make jet planes, they don't build any more propeller planes as they did twenty years ago. But in literature there isn't such a thing as collective progress. One man may go far; another stands in one place. In literature today, you will find a man who is five hundred years backward and in some cases even five thousand . . . We cannot make any generalizations, because literature and creative art are generally dependent on genes and their evolution is unknown to us. No one can predict biological mutations.

BURGIN: If I might return to the question of religion—you've said that you've always believed in God. Yet you have the capacity to envision with enormous vitality and verisimilitude characters who are skeptics. In fact, I think of your characters Zipkin, Ezriel, and Lucian in *The Estate* as examples of deviating from belief in God, each to a different degree. How is it that you're able to imagine this so clearly?

SINGER: Since there is no evidence attesting to what God is, I doubt all the time, as I told you. So I dramatize in these characters my own doubt. Actually, doubt is part of all religion. All religious thinkers were doubters. Even the Bible, although it is full of faith, is also full of skepticism. The Book of Job you can call a Book of Skepticism.

In the Book of Psalms, man says to God, "Why do you sleep, God? Why don't you wake up and see what's happening?" Lovers are sometimes full of suspicion and even hostility towards the person they love. The girl who loves you will ask you ten times a day, "Do you really love me?" You always have to say, "Yes, yes, yes!" The same thing is true in religion. I believe in God, I also doubt. I have moments when I think maybe the atheist Feuerbach was right.

BURGIN: I remember you said to me, "Well, if the world is a jungle, that's the way God wanted it." When we were talking about "little people" who had so much power, I said, "How can God allow this?" You said, "Maybe God is a little God."

SINGER: I am not a man who *preaches* religion. My religion is for myself. I have moments when I almost deny God but I also have moments of religious exultation. When I'm in trouble, I pray. And because I'm in trouble all of the time, I pray almost constantly.

Religion is not a simple thing and neither is love. You can love a woman and still betray her. In my belief in God there's only one thing which is steady: I never say that the universe was an accident. The word "accident" should be erased from the dictionary. It has some meaning in everyday life but no meaning in philosophy.

10.

A little island . . . The limits of philosophy
. . . Experiments in free choice . . .
A true protester

BURGIN: When we were talking about Nabokov you mentioned that although you have mixed feelings about him, you were relieved to discover that he believed in the supernatural. I wonder what you mean by that term, "supernatural."

SINGER: I don't really believe that there are two things —the natural and the supernatural. I would not say that gravity is natural and telepathy is supernatural. If telepathy exists, it has as much right to call itself natural as gravitation does. We call the things which we don't know or for which we have no evidence supernatural. For example, there is no real evidence that there is a soul or that there is free will. The same applies to ghosts or spirits or other entities whose existence we cannot prove.

Can we prove that there is such a thing as love? There are a number of people who will tell you that love is nothing but carnal desire. Some extreme behaviorists don't believe that there is such a thing as inborn character or personality. They say everything is conditioned, except for a few instincts like the fear of loud noise or falling. Now, for thousands and thousands of years men married women and had children, and the fathers called themselves fathers even though there was no scientific evidence that they were the fathers, since there were cases where they were not. Still, most of the people who have a wife and children believe that they are the fathers of the children. Although Strindberg wrote a play, *The Father,* in which he tried to show that no man can really maintain that he is the father of his children, we know that in most cases, especially in former times, women were faithful. What I want to emphasize by this is that the supernatural is only a word for things whose existence we can't yet prove.

BURGIN: That reminds me of a saying of Conrad's that the real world is so fantastic that in a sense there's no difference between the so-called supernatural world and the real one.

SINGER: Yes, we still don't know what magnetism is and why a magnet will attract a nail and not cottage cheese. The atom is more of a riddle today than it was three thousand years ago. We don't know really what light is. We don't know what life is. We speak of electrons and we know how they work, more or less, but not what they are and how they came to be. Actually, our knowledge is a little island in an infinite ocean of nonknowledge. And even this little island remains a riddle.

BURGIN: When you affirm the so-called supernatural, are you saying, "I'm trying in my writing to call attention to the fact of how little we really know"?

SINGER: You have expressed exactly my way of thinking. I try to call attention to the things which we cannot prove but in whose existence some of us still believe.

BURGIN: Socrates said, "I know nothing except the fact of my ignorance."

SINGER: When it comes to these things, no one can be original because of our common ignorance. Originality is not the only important quality of a writer. Sometimes we have to repeat emotions and ideas because we cannot function without them. If a man is in love with a woman and says, "I love you," he knows very well that millions of people have said it before. But this word "love" is, for the time being, adequate and it expresses more or less what he feels. There are people who are original by nature. They use phrases which have been used many times but the sum total of what they say or write creates a feeling of originality. There are also writers who try to make every sentence original; they don't allow themselves to write a single sentence unless it has some queerness—and the net result is banality. Now, Tolstoy was an original man, even though he begins *Anna Karenina* with a saying which is quite banal. When you finish *Anna Karenina* or *War and Peace* or his other works, you feel here is an original person. There are other writers about whom you feel that there is nothing original in them. All you can see is the frustrated ambition to be original all the time.

BURGIN: Can you think of any such writers?

SINGER: I can think of such writers but I'm not going to mention names.

BURGIN: How did your interest in the supernatural develop? Can you trace it to its source?

SINGER: I was interested in the supernatural all my life. I knew even as a child that the world which we see is not the whole world. Whether you call them demons or angels or some other name, I knew then, and I know today, that there are entities of whom we have no idea and they do exist. You can call them spirits, ghosts, or imps. Of course, I also use them as symbols in my writing. I can express with them many things which would be difficult for me to express if I only wrote about people. But it is not only a literary method, it is connected with a belief that the world is full of powers that we don't know. After all, let's not fool ourselves, a few hundred years ago we didn't know about microbes, we didn't know about electrons and all those powers connected with radiation. So who says that we have already come to the summit of knowledge?

BURGIN: On the other hand, we're learning or we think we're learning more about microbes and electrons, but where can it be proved that we've learned or discovered anything at all about the spirit world? Our knowledge of it doesn't progress.

SINGER: It's not something with which you can progress. When it comes to human character or to ethics we don't progress.

BURGIN: But if these entities exist, why have we learned nothing definite about them?

SINGER: Because they are not made to be discovered. And the reason is that if we did discover them, free choice would disappear, and I think that free choice is such a great gift of God that if it disappeared it would be a profound misfortune. It would finish human history. If we could prove that there is a God and there is a Satan and that there is connected with them a world of punishment and reward, free choice would completely disappear. All people would be afraid of these powers, they would act accordingly, and it would do away with man's struggle. Because of this, I don't think you can ever take these powers into a laboratory and demonstrate them. Although I like to do in my own way a little research to prove certain things to myself, I know that no final proof can ever come as long as humanity is going in the direction in which it is going. The moment people began to investigate the physical world one discovery came after the other, and they will continue to come for maybe a million years from now. But when it comes to these things—the existence of God, Providence, free will, and so on—no discovery could ever come which would convince us once and forever.

BURGIN: When I spoke with you a couple of days ago you were emphasizing that the primary purpose of literature is entertainment—its level of entertainment depending, of course, on the audience one is writing for. But I was a little confused about your view of the purpose of philosophy.

SINGER: Philosophy is a kind of learning in which you really have to believe. There are no proofs, as in exact science. Spinoza has not proven that there is a Substance with an infinite number of attributes. But you can still say, "I believe in Spinoza. I love his way of thinking." When Schopenhauer said that the thing-in-itself is will, he believed that he had found some truth. All philosophers are in a sense dealing with the truth of their belief.

BURGIN: Do you feel that philosophy may have nowhere to go, in fact may have no real future and may simply dissolve?

SINGER: At the beginning, the philosophers believed in the power of logic. Then came critical philosophy and it told us that logic is all definition and nothing else. It can never cross those limits.

BURGIN: The limits as Kant defined them.

SINGER: Not only Kant, also Locke and Hume. Kant came after them. Then there was a revival of metaphysics—as in Hegel, who tried again with the power of definition and logic to create something. Lately such philosophers as Wittgenstein and others tried to turn philosophy into a discipline of language. Sometimes philosophy looks as if it would be at the very end of its efforts.

BURGIN: Perhaps that kind of man is dying out?

SINGER: But to say that philosophy is finished would be too much guesswork, because we never know what will come. There may suddenly come a man who may be another Spinoza or another Descartes or another Leibnitz. I feel that since the desire of human beings is to know, and since this hunger is still with us, we cannot say that philosophy has been finished.

BURGIN: So you've moved away from the position of at least partially aligning philosophy with science?

SINGER: While it pretends to be a science, it's actually a part of human character, of the way human beings think and feel. It has to be repetitious, just as the human spirit is.

BURGIN: I'm curious *how* you read philosophy, assuming you still do.

SINGER: I seldom do.

BURGIN: Well, when you've most recently read philosophy how do you read it? As a curious branch of literature?

SINGER: I know now that nothing the philosophers have said and are now saying and perhaps nothing they are going to say in the future ever can have the kind of evidence which one can have in physics or in chemistry. We have to make peace with this. People have tried to find absolute truth and failed.

BURGIN: But they're still interesting failures to read . . .

SINGER: Yes, and they will continue to try and they will continue to fail. It's the fault of the discipline.

BURGIN: Do you feel that perhaps Kant came as close as a philosopher can come towards making an empirical case for his categories of understanding when he says our minds are constructed to perceive time and space the way they are? That seems almost irrefutable.

SINGER: It has been shown by Salomon Maimon and the neo-Kantians that even existence is nothing but a category of thinking. We cannot say that there *is* a thing-in-itself, because perhaps existence itself is only a way of thinking, not being. It's good that all these philosophers have finally made us realize that "reality" is only reality from our point of view, from the point of view of our senses, of our consciousness. They have destroyed many illusions, but they have never created anything positive. Spinoza, who tried to give us something positive, ended up with something that became nothing but an arbitrary definition. His Substance with its infinite attributes is only a game of words. We just don't know what a piece of wood is if we take away man's perceptions of it. Since we are imprisoned by our senses and by our way of thinking and this prison will last as long as we live, we have to make peace with it and deal with things in this "prison," as Plotinus and Philo called the body and the senses.

BURGIN: How do you reconcile this with your belief in free will?

SINGER: Of course, I cannot prove that it exists, but I prefer to believe that there is free choice. And in my own way, I make experiments with free choice. I sometimes want to convince myself how free I am. Can I make a decision and keep it or can't I? Because all my life I made, God knows, myriads of decisions and I broke so many of them.

BURGIN: What do you mean?

SINGER: For example, I made a decision to get up at eight o'clock in the morning and I got up at ten o'clock instead. In Warsaw, almost every day I made a decision not to waste my time in the writers' club, take part in the gossip and immediately I went there and wasted my time in talking nonsense. Even now, in my old age, I try again and again to make decisions and keep them, hoping against hope that it is not too late and that I may succeed one day. Hope and the idea of free will are entities which one cannot give up completely.

The truth is, I have been wasting time since I grew up, but somehow I succeeded in doing a little work. I would say that wasting time is my passion Number Two, and the feeling of guilt for wasting time is my sickness Number Three. To me, this feeling of guilt proves that I really believe in free choice.

BURGIN: Aren't there some areas of life where you are reacting according to nature, not really consciously making a decision?

SINGER: I don't need to make a decision to eat breakfast. When I say making a decision, I mean making a decision *against* my desires. The Ten Commandments are commandments against human nature. Many people would like to steal if they knew that they could do it without being punished. It is also their nature to commit adultery if they can have their way without too much trouble. But Moses came and he said that if humanity wants to exist it has to follow certain rules no matter how difficult they are. I would say that even to this day we have not yet convinced ourselves that people can make such decisions and keep them. Even when they make them, they can only keep them if they make them as a collective. If people live together like the Jews in the ghettos they keep to their decisions. Why? Because one guards the other. In a collective, if a Jew wanted to commit adultery, there were many in the little ghetto who would have learned about it and they would have made a great outcry to stop it. There was a case where Tolstoy in his old age got a strong desire for some peasant woman and he went to a friend and said, "Please do me a favor and guard me." This means he knew that by himself he didn't have enough free will to take care of himself. These are the problems which interest me deeply.

BURGIN: You mentioned that you often feel you are wasting time. What do you consider *not* wasting time?

SINGER: When I speak about wasting time, I don't speak from a philosophical point of view but from a practical one. I assume that if I get up in the morning and do my work, three or four hours, and I accomplish something, write a story which I can later sell or which I will enjoy having published, I haven't wasted my time. But if I get up in the morning and I read yesterday's newspaper or look out the window for hours, or have a long telephone conversation of no value, this is wasting time. Of course, it is relative, but I'm not speaking here from a philosophical point of view. Like every writer, I would like to do my work well, to write and rewrite, but when I neglect my job, I feel that I have broken my decision. This is why when we betray our decisions, we all have these regrets. The word "regret" itself shows that we assume that we have some free will, because if we didn't believe in free will, we wouldn't regret anything.

BURGIN: I'm wondering if you ever feel that everything is a waste of time. And if so, why is the practice of literature, which, in your view, only serves to entertain people, more important than entertaining yourself or entertaining writers with conversation in a writers' club?

SINGER: Well, it has a pragmatic value.

BURGIN: We've talked quite a bit about philosophy, but there is one last question I'd like to ask you about it. What can a fiction writer gain, if anything, from a study of philosophy?

SINGER: If the novelist is not curious about philosophy, there is no reason why he should read philosophy. But he is never curious about philosophy, even when he's young. This shows there's something small about him. A larger person is interested in the so-called eternal questions: Who am I? Is what we see reality? Is there any way of reaching *true* reality? If he sits down to read philosophy because he thinks that a writer should know philosophy, I'd tell him, "Don't read it." If he's a real writer and a thinking man, he will be curious about it and maybe, after a while, disappointed in it. He will say, "I've had enough of it," and return from abstraction to the world of the senses.

BURGIN: How can a novelist effectively use ideas? For example, Dostoyevsky dramatized philosophical ideas. How have you yourself used them?

SINGER: I would say if he needs them in his stories, if he is the kind of writer who likes to write about ideas, he can find a million ways of using them.

BURGIN: How have you used them?

SINGER: Since I often describe people like myself and I am interested in human ideas, I let my people ponder the eternal questions. I could never make the protagonist of a novel a person who would not be interested in those questions. In other words, I don't make use of philosophy with a pertinent scheme or plan. Those writers who imagined that they found the final answer were sooner or later a disappointment to others and often to themselves. In my time, Tolstoy could serve as the example par excellence. There is no question that he died a disappointed man. His disenchantment would have been greater if he had lived to see the Bolshevist Revolution. Just the same, I have great admiration for him and for his struggle with God and with human nature.

I myself try to think that I have made peace with human blindness and God's permanent silence, but they give me no rest. I feel a deep resentment against the Almighty. My religion goes hand in hand with a profound feeling of protest. Once in a while, the old Jewish hope for the coming of the Messiah awakens in me. There must come the time for revelation! How long should we wait? My feeling of religion is a feeling of rebellion. I even play with the idea of creating (for myself) a religion of protest. I often say to myself that God *wants* us to protest. He has had enough of those who praise Him all the time and bless Him for all His cruelties to man and animals.

I have written a little book which I call *Rebellion and Prayer* or *The True Protester*. It is still in Yiddish, untranslated. It was written at the time of the Holocaust. It is a bitter little book and I doubt that I will ever publish it. Yes, I am a troubled person, but I am also joyful when I forget (for a while) the mess in which we are stuck. I may be false and contradictory in many ways, but I am a true protester. If I could, I would picket the Almighty with a sign: "Unfair to Life."

11.

Singer's stories . . . The female narrator
. . . Rationalists and believers . . . Mystic
realism . . . Every story has its problems
. . . The artist and the scientist

BURGIN: Let me ask you some questions about your short stories. Unlike most male writers, you often have women as narrators. Do you *feel* differently when you create a female narrator?

SINGER: I use the female narrator because among the Yiddish-speaking people the storytellers were either the Hassidim or the old women. They used to sit there on the porches of their houses and tell stories. And since they were not inhibited by special doubts, they would just say whatever they had to say in their own way and they said it sometimes in a very picturesque and remarkable manner. I usually use the monologue of some Hassid or of some old woman. Of course, in my stories I also use monologues of people who come to ask "advice" from me. I often let people tell their stories in their own way, instead of my sitting there and telling their stories in my voice. It's both very convenient and very fruitful to let people tell their own stories.

BURGIN: Do you believe that there is a female part to each man or a male part to each woman?

SINGER: Yes, there's no question that the male is not one hundred percent male and the female is not one hundred percent female. We have so much in common. Of course, men and women are very different, but they are also very much alike.

BURGIN: Some people have trouble when they try to actually pinpoint the differences. What are the differences besides the biological ones?

SINGER: They are mostly biological, but also psychological. The female is less of a doubter. She may not have the need to say *cogito ergo sum.* She knows that she exists. Actually, that is why many of the storytellers in my works are old women. And many of them believe in the supernatural. They don't think they are talking about mere fantasy. To let them talk is very good from a literary point of view. I would say the majority of stories I tell myself, but a substantial part of them are monologues of imaginary women. They add credibility to the story.

BURGIN: You've emphasized that you try to write with models from life.

SINGER: Always.

BURGIN: On what did you base your stories that are set in poorhouses? What was the model for those stories?

SINGER: There was a poorhouse in the town of Bilgoray where my grandfather lived.

BURGIN: Why would you go there?

SINGER: I liked to go in and hear people tell stories and also some beggars used to come and sleep in the study house and they told stories, too. In these towns in Poland storytelling was really a part of life, because people did not read newspapers, very few people read books in those small towns. Storytelling was their literature, their theater, their movies, and their TV. Stories have been told by people since man became what he is, since he developed a language.

BURGIN: In your stories you've often emphasized the contradictory forces at war within people. One of these characters who most intrigued me is Dr. Beeber from the story of the same name. How would you describe the conflicts that he suffered from?

SINGER: I don't remember that he suffered from conflicts. I remember that he was a woman chaser . . .

BURGIN: Yes, but he also had needs within himself which created a conflict. He was worried about keeping up a certain style of life, he was worried about money, so he married a woman who satisfied those needs, and he seemed to be happy and then he destroyed it all in one night.

SINGER: The saying that man kills what he loves is very much true. Not only does he kill his love, he very often kills his business or career.

BURGIN: You've written about that theme quite a bit, I think.

SINGER: I think all writers do.

BURGIN: In your story "Caricature" you have a line where Dr. Margolis says, "Old age is merely a parody of one's youth." Can you elaborate on that?

SINGER: There's nothing to elaborate. I think it would fit him to say so.

BURGIN: You wouldn't say it as a general law?

SINGER: No, it's not a general law. It fits him to say that in this particular situation. I don't try to make everything that my characters say Newtonian laws which are valid all over the world and in the whole cosmos. For my particular purpose they are valid. Let's say a man quarrels with his wife and says, "All women are terrible." That doesn't mean that all women are terrible. While he is quarreling with his wife, he says so; when he makes peace with her, he may say something else. He may say, "I love women." It is true that the critics would like to make from every little thing which a writer lets his heroes say some kind of a law, to regulate it and make it be valid forever, but it's a big mistake.

BURGIN: "The Shadow of a Crib" is one of your few stories where the protagonist is not Jewish. Why did you decide to make Yarzetsky a Gentile?

SINGER: Why not? I also know Catholic people.

BURGIN: But you so rarely write about Gentiles. Couldn't he have been one of your heretical or non-believing Jews?

SINGER: No, this story had to be among Gentiles. Jews in those times did not fall in love this way, and they didn't have a Ball. All these things had to be Russian or Polish.

BURGIN: Do you feel less secure when you write about a character who isn't Jewish?

SINGER: No, as a matter of fact they've just translated my novels *The Manor* and *The Estate* into Polish, and they like them there very much. In those novels I describe Poles. If I had described Poles in a false way, the critics there would tear me to pieces, but they seem to like them. I know not only Jews but Poles and Russians. I could even write about American people. The only thing is, since they speak English and I write in Yiddish, I don't like, really, to make them speak in a translated language. But I have lived in this country longer than I have lived in Poland, and I had girlfriends here and other friends who spoke to me in English. I wouldn't say that I know Americans better than, let's say, Jack London knew them, but those Americans whom I know, I know.

BURGIN: I'm interested in discussing some of the themes and connections that occur in your story "The Séance." The protagonist of that story, Kalisher, is a failed rationalist, a skeptic, who keeps company with a bogus mystic Mrs. Kopitsky. You make fun of her in a way and yet she emerges as a kind of savior of his so that we take her last words about living and loving forever a little seriously too. Can you remember what your attitude towards your characters was and what you were generally trying to express in that story?

SINGER: I was trying to express the conflict between the believer and the rationalist. He is a rationalist and therefore doubts or doesn't believe at all in the supernatural. As a rationalist he can see very well that she's a faker. But just the same, the rationalist, while he's very clever in his field, has no real understanding of the believer. A rationalist like Kalisher is not a believer, and not being a believer, he cannot understand this woman. Although she's faking from a rational point of view, she may be telling the truth from the believer's point of view. In other words, if the believer says that he has had a revelation, he's lying. He didn't have a revelation, but the "revelation" itself may contain truth which a rationalist would deny because he has no real touch with the believer's world.

BURGIN: Also in "The Séance," in his moment of deepest despair, Kalisher wets his pants. I notice that image in a number of your stories. For example, the Rabbi in the story "Something Is There" needs to urinate and he can't. Are you dramatizing a connection between body and mind, how the body breaks down when the spirit is broken?

SINGER: Yes. There is an instinctive belief that the mind and the body are connected, more connected than experiments can show. When a person resigns, the body also resigns. The heart begins to resign, the stomach begins to resign, the sex organs begin to resign.

BURGIN: You also end the story with a situation that recurs in a number of your stories—namely, a woman coming to the rescue of an ailing intellectual man who might otherwise die without her. Was this a feeling that you were also trying to convey in the story "Neighbors"? I mean the idea of a mutual need between characters of opposite disposition and viewpoints?

SINGER: Yes. When they come together they act in a way of mutual help. Actually, she helps him. I think she's in a carriage and he pulls the carriage. They create a kind of completion between instinct and rationalism.

BURGIN: Does the title and thrust of that story try to underscore that apparent opposites are actually neighbors in the human soul?

SINGER: I will tell you . . . when I sit down to write, I don't say to myself, "I am trying to show this." I don't really know what I'm going to try; I let the story work for itself. These questions of yours are rationalistic kinds of questions. "What is your purpose? What did you intend to do?" Of course I have a purpose, I want to write a story, but I don't say to myself before I write the story, "This story is going to teach you such and such," because if I did this, the story would never come out. I let the story go its own way and bring out its own results. While I am in a way controlling it, I don't create it with a plan. And even after I've done it, I'm not a hundred percent sure what I've done and how it can be explained. It's like when you have a child. You don't know if it's going to be a boy or a girl, or whether this child is going to marry and bring you a grandchild, or is going to do something else. When you read the Book of Genesis, it tells the story of Adam and Eve and the serpent. If you would have asked the question "What do you want to bring out?" you would probably hear: "This is the way I dreamed it" or "This is the way it was revealed to me." The answer would not be really a rationalistic answer or a logical answer. The reason would be that he didn't know himself what was going on. What was really going on in that story is that no creature except man is ashamed of himself, criticizes himself, tries to deny himself, is ashamed of his nakedness. Can you imagine a dog or a cow or a bird being ashamed of its nakedness? They are not ashamed because they are at peace with nature, at peace with the Creator, while man is not. But the man who wrote this couldn't have said all this. He just wrote it that way, and wrote in a few lines profound ideas which people have not yet discovered, or still have to discover.

BURGIN: But still, the writing you do isn't automatic writing. You still have to ultimately make all kinds of aesthetic decisions.

SINGER: I have to control it. But I don't control it in a way where the purpose comes first and the actual work later. Actually, the work and the purpose go together.

BURGIN: For example, one decision that you had to make in the story "The Letter Writer" was when Rose Beechem visits Herman. You make a reference to the fact that she avoids touching the ink blotter as if she were telepathically aware of Herman's mystic experience. When you make a decision to make a description of that nature you're creating an attitude, aren't you?

You're suggesting that it's possible that this experience had an objective basis and really happened.

SINGER: Yes. I think it's what you'd call ambiguous. The story should have both a logical explanation and at the same time a *mystic* explanation.

BURGIN: I think another story where you do that is "The Cafeteria."

SINGER: In all of my writings I remain ambiguous. The reason for the ambiguity is that since I write for modern man and he is a rationalist, I cannot tell him that this is the perfect truth, but neither do I want to tell him that this is a perfect lie. I make it so that it can be explained in two ways.

BURGIN: In "The Cafeteria," there's a psychological explanation for why Esther sees the dead people.

SINGER: There is a psychological reason, but at the same time I make the man who has heard this story think that maybe she really did see something.

BURGIN: He sees her walking with someone who may well be dead.

SINGER: Yes. In other words, it has to be right on two levels. Very few mystic writers do this. In most cases, either they stand completely on the side of mysticism or they stand completely on the side of rationalism. But you know who didn't? Edgar Allan Poe. In Poe's stories you can always explain him rationally by saying to yourself, "Well, the man was a maniac, he was crazy, he imagined all these things." But at the same time when you read them you have the feeling that there is some truth in them, or the possibility of a truth.

BURGIN: I'm surprised you're not put off by the ornateness of his style.

SINGER: He didn't write with the style of a realist. When he wrote his story he said in effect, "You have to believe it or not." In my case, I try to imbue my story with realism. I try to write it in such a way that if it would have really happened, this is the way it would have been. In other words, it's a form of mystic realism.

BURGIN: You seldom use contemporary historical references in your stories.

SINGER: Almost never.

BURGIN: So when you do I'm naturally curious about how much of the story is based on fact. I'm thinking of your reference to Einstein in "The Joke." I'm curious to know if there was really a Dr. Walden who was a friend of Einstein. And did Einstein really come to his funeral? How much of that story was based on events in your life?

SINGER: It was based on some fact. I knew a man, maybe he's still alive, who used to write letters to an intellectual celebrity of sorts in Russia. He wanted to receive letters from a number of so-called celebrities and he felt that if he took an old man, and wrote to him as a girl who is in love with him, the man would answer. So this is what he did. He did it with a purpose. Of course, the desire to get letters from these celebrities was in itself neither very clear nor logical. But once he decided to do it he cultivated his correspondence logically. From this little thing which this man told me I created this story. Here is a man, although he's a clever man and in a way a great man, who is fooled by this scheme of the letter writer. And then Einstein, who is, so to say, a symbol of rationalism, comes to his funeral.

BURGIN: Was that part pure invention?

SINGER: It could have happened. Since he comes from Berlin they might have known each other, and he *could* have come to his funeral.

BURGIN: When you occasionally refer to members of your family in your stories, are we then to assume that these instances are part of your biography?

SINGER: When it comes to my family, I don't need to invent.

BURGIN: Do you then have different "rules" for yourself when you use members of your family in your stories? For example, in "Three Encounters" you quote your mother several times. Are we to assume this was actual dialogue from your life?

SINGER: It is true. I knew exactly how my mother would have spoken in such a case. I'm realistic. If my mother would have really been there, and if this would have happened, this is exactly how my mother would have expressed herself. In other words, while I may write a completely supernatural story, I try to make it as realistic as possible. This adds power to the mystical story, because even a mystical story should have realism. For example, the Bible tells us that when Moses saw a burning bush he understood that God wanted to talk to him. This is fine. But when Moses saw a burning bush, this bush was burning in a realistic way. He really saw a bush, and he saw it burn. If I read about a man who sees a burning bush and the fire went sideways instead of up, it would distort the reality of the fire and weaken the mysticism of the story. The more you give a story realistic power, the more you enhance its mystical power, too.

BURGIN: I'm curious about how you happened to write the story "Powers." There's a story that seems to be modeled on your early days as a journalist. I'm wondering if you knew such a man or if that story was completely invented?

SINGER: People have told me stories but not exactly like this one.

BURGIN: It's a composite of fact and invention?

SINGER: Yes, it's always a composite. I take my own convictions, my own feelings, but I try to describe them in such a way that they sound as if they really happened, so that you are able to ask me, "Did it really happen?" If it were written differently you wouldn't even ask me this question. You would know from reading it that it couldn't have happened.

BURGIN: Some stories you write don't deal with supernatural themes at all. Do you feel your imagination is

working differently with a different set of problems in
those stories?

SINGER: I would say every story has its problems. You
don't write stories according to a recipe or to a ready-
made plan. The story "The Little Shoemakers" has a
different approach than "Gimpel the Fool." "The Little
Shoemakers" is a realistic kind of story. Of course, it is
not completely realistic. But still, it almost could be
realistic. This old shoemaker could have come to America. This is true of every story. Each time a writer's
situation is different and he works differently. And this
is true also in human relations as well. For instance,
when you meet a girl, you get a feeling how to talk to
her. You will talk to her differently than you would talk
to another girl.

BURGIN: So you're comparing that to how you approach different stories?

SINGER: Yes. With one girl you will speak in a casual
way, but you will speak differently to a girl if you feel
she's a fancy creature. You do this completely by instinct. You don't say to yourself, "I'm going to talk to her
differently than I spoke to the girl I met yesterday." You
do it.

BURGIN: Two stories that I associate with each other
are "The Cabalist of East Broadway" and "Vanvild
Kava."

SINGER: "The Cabalist of East Broadway" is almost a
true story. I describe a man who did indeed go to Israel,

but I'm not sure whether he came back. I think he went there and died there.

Burgin: In that story the hero renounces "the good life" in Israel.

Singer: First he runs away and then he comes back and we don't know the reason and because we don't know the reason we believe that it happened, because people of this kind are terribly unpredictable. And this unpredictability is more convincing than if he acted in a "logical way."

Burgin: This story is somewhat like "Vanvild Kava." Kava has a chance to be published and destroys it for no apparent reason.

Singer: Yes, a person like Kava is capable of this. By the way, that is almost a true story.

Burgin: Self-destruction or the renunciation of the world's riches is a theme that runs through a lot of your work. I wonder why that theme appeals to you so much.

Singer: The world is full of it. As a matter of fact, the whole human race is a self-destructive race. When you read now about Lebanon it just seems that here is a group of people who do one thing—they do just what the lemmings do—they go into the ocean and drown. They just destroy themselves—they only need an excuse.

Burgin: There's sort of a kamikaze in every human brain?

SINGER: Oh, yes. Very much so.

BURGIN: Another theme that interests me in your writing is the ambivalent quality of sex—that it's both life-giving and destructive. I'm thinking in particular now of your story "A Quotation from Klopstock." In that story, sex brings both life and death to Theresa.

SINGER: Here is a man who has no reason to make love to this woman. He wanted just to be friendly or polite.

BURGIN: But do you believe anybody would do that just to be polite? Didn't it gratify him on some level?

SINGER: Yes. A feeling of pity, and also at the same time maybe it was mixed with a love of adventure. To sometimes do the impossible or the ridiculous is appealing. Freud, with all his knowledge, with all his insight, was a rationalist. He tried to create formulas like the Oedipus complex and the Electra complex. The moment you create formulas you already stray from artistic truth.

BURGIN: When you read Freud, do you feel that he's distorting human life?

SINGER: No, he's not distorting it. There is a lot of truth in Freud. But what he does is to take one case and say that it works everywhere, whereas in reality there isn't such a thing.

BURGIN: But all men resemble each other, we're all part of the same species.

SINGER: Actually, when it comes to real truth one case never resembles another. Let's say you will find twenty people who really destroyed themselves. But just investigate and look into their lives and you will see that similar as they were, they were very much different. Of course, if you give castor oil to twenty people they will all run to the toilet, because this is the way castor oil works.

BURGIN: But there are some basic things in all people, such as a will to live.

SINGER: A will to live is in every human being, but each person will go about it in a completely different way.

BURGIN: Don't you think that a sexual desire is also in every human being?

SINGER: Yes, it is in every human being, but let's say a woman will have in her life twenty men. She will tell you that every one of them was very much different, and this difference is just as strong as the similarities. Of course, the scientist, even if he's a psychologist, will only tell you a case history. He wants to make from one case a kind of a rule or a law that this Oedipus complex didn't happen to just one particular man but that there are millions of men with the same complex.

BURGIN: That's where you part company.

SINGER: The artist is satisfied to say, "This happened to this particular man." It's almost a fact that Newton discovered the idea of gravitation from a falling apple.

Now, an artist would have said, "Here is a peculiar kind of an apple. When it goes off the tree it falls." He wouldn't have discovered that this happens to all apples. He would have described with as much art as he could what happened to this single apple and that would have been enough for him. But Newton, being a scientist, said to himself, "What happened to this apple will happen to all apples, it happens to the planets, it happens to the rivers." He made it a law. I am satisfied with the individual apple. This is the difference between the artist and the scientist. The artist is not eager to create a rule. He wants to show individuality, he's interested in what is unique. But the scientist, no matter how much he admires uniqueness, wants to make the unique non-unique. This is his work. If he does not reach it, he thinks he fails. If Newton had found that gravitation happened only to this particular apple, he would have lost all interest.

BURGIN: But let's consider a writer whom I know you admire, Dostoyevsky. He was very interested in unique situations, but also in ideas.

SINGER: He was interested in ideas, but he managed to use the ideas in unique cases. Take, for example, Raskolnikov. Of course, Dostoyevsky's novel *Crime and Punishment* has a scientific title. It sounds like it could have been a book by a sociologist writing about crime and about punishment, but only the title is scientific. It could not have taken place in China or even anywhere else in Russia. It was the single case of a murderer and this is what makes it so great. If Raskolnikov would really express all murderers, it would then be either a scientific work or a worthless work—most probably worthless, because it would still not be scientific. Everything which Raskolnikov says and does is something which no other murderers say or do. Because it is unique, it is so true, and because it is so true, it has also in a way a profound scientific value.

BURGIN: That's kind of a paradox.

SINGER: There is no such thing as a murderer who resembles all other murderers. If you describe a murderer who resembles other murderers, you describe an idea, not a real case. For an event to be true it must not resemble any other event.

BURGIN: So from your point of view the only way a fiction writer should use ideas is to reveal the character's psychology, as opposed to making any statements about life that might have an objective validity or interest.

SINGER: I say that the less the protagonist resembles other people, the more true it is. The more it resembles other people, the less truth it will have. This is the reason why comparative literature is basically going to wither away. Because if you can compare it, then it's not literature.

BURGIN: Since we've been talking about rationalism and the supernatural and communication between the mind and the body, I'd like to ask you about those stories where you suggest some kind of communication between people and animals. For example, in "The Letter" Herman has a relationship with a mouse.

SINGER: You don't find many men who will leave a little milk and a piece of cheese for a mouse. You know that most men, almost all of them, will try to get a cat or else rat poison and kill it. Here is a unique case. To say that Herman is a symbol of humanity would be completely false. The only thing we can learn from him is that just because he was so unique it all sounds true.

BURGIN: I wonder if you could comment on another of your animal stories, "The Young Heifer."

SINGER: A unique story.

BURGIN: That story really sounds like it came from your life.

SINGER: Yes. I once saw a heifer scream like this and a man told me that it had been taken out from a stable where there were other cows and the heifer was missing either its mother or its home. This was true. However, I attached this screaming heifer to my life and it became a unique case. You cannot try to write another story about a screaming heifer. It would be an imitation and meaningless. Still, the most peculiar thing is that the more a person is unique, the more he resembles others. That is the paradox of life.

12.

The story is the message . . . The mood of the ghetto . . . There are no guarantees . . . *Shosha* and its atmosphere

BURGIN: How would you characterize your aims in your novel *Shosha?*

SINGER: My aim was and always is to tell a story which is *my* story. *Shosha* is a love story between a so-called normal man and an abnormal woman, half retarded or whatever you would call her. I never have any other aim when I sit down to write a story except the story itself. The story *is* the aim. If I see a good story and it's *my* story, I write it. First of all, no other writer I know lived on Krochmalna Street in this period. No writer whom I know was in love with someone like Shosha. It was my story. If I have, as I said many times, a topic for the story and a desire to write the story, and I'm convinced that it's my story, I don't worry about the message. If I have the choice between a message and a story, I always take the story and let the message go to hell. If you would ask me what kind of message there is in this story, I would say, I don't see the message. What is the message? That a man liked the girlfriend of his youth in spite of the fact that she was half retarded? There is simply no message in it. What was the name of the scholar who said that the media is the message or something like that . . .

BURGIN: Marshall McLuhan.

SINGER: Yes. I would say the story *is* the message. When Tolstoy wrote *Anna Karenina* the message was already written before by Flaubert in *Madame Bovary*. In both cases the woman betrayed her husband and she suffered and she committed suicide. So as far as the message is concerned there is no originality in *Anna Karenina*. But the originality is in the story, the *story* is different, the writing.

BURGIN: Would it be overinterpreting to say that one "message" in *Shosha* is that all systems or messages are inadequate in light of the mysteries or complexities of life?

SINGER: I think it's the critic or the good reader who should find the message if he is after it. I personally can like literature without finding messages and symbols in every story I read.

BURGIN: I don't mean a moral message but a kind of theme beyond the story.

SINGER: In *Shosha* there are people who are going to be destroyed and they don't know why they are going to be destroyed and what the purpose of this is.

BURGIN: They try to rationalize the inexplicable.

SINGER: Also, here are rich people, people who could have escaped and they don't escape.

BURGIN: In that way your method is a bit akin to Dostoyevsky's in *Crime and Punishment,* because there the mystery isn't who committed the murder, but why did he do it? In *Shosha* it is not who does Aaron marry, but why does he make this decision?

SINGER: We never know why people choose one person or another.

BURGIN: You told me that frugality was a guiding principle in constructing *Shosha.*

SINGER: Yes. I have said to myself many times that one of the wonderful things about the Book of Genesis and the Bible generally is that the stories there are very, very short—so short that even a short short story today would be too long in comparison. Often a story is told in five or six sentences. I said to myself that modern literature suffers terribly from verbosity. No matter what they tell you, they tell it to you again and again and it makes it so that there's no place left for the reader's imagination. In the Bible, so much is left to the reader that actually the story is but a hint and the rest is for the reader to finish. I don't mean that you should make things short when you have to tell a lot, but to give the essentials, and leave as much as possible to the imagination of the reader. I would say that I tried this method in all my short stories, but as far as a novel is concerned, well, I wanted to say that *Shosha* is the first time, but it's not true. *Satan in Goray* is also very short and so are some of my other books.

BURGIN: From talking with your secretary, I learned that when you were doing the editing of *Shosha* there were many more pages than those which actually appeared in the final book.

SINGER: Very many.

BURGIN: Which kinds of sections or scenes did you cut out?

SINGER: I cut out many things which I thought were not really essential. *Shosha* is the only novel I've written in the first person. It's almost like a memoir. It is a novel of understatement because the literary style of today is overstatement—you make from a molehill a mountain. In *Shosha* I do the opposite. The Hitler tragedy is a mountain that cannot be seen as it was. It has to be reduced to a small number of episodes. Events which could be made into a big drama I tell in only a sentence, because the drama which came after this, the Holocaust, was of such magnitude that it was beyond the pale of literature.

Although the characters in *Shosha* don't live in a ghetto, the mood of the ghetto is stronger than in my other works because these people live on the edge of a volcano that has not yet erupted but may do so any moment. They live in a quiet despair, not in a raging despair. They never intended to fight back. They were just waiting and trying to forget, by making love, reading books, speaking about some nonexistent hope. They enjoyed the kind of peace that comes with utter resignation. Some of them acquired a childish confidence and carelessness.

BURGIN: Speaking of the Yiddish mood of the ghetto, I read an interview in which you touched on the special character of the Yiddish man of the ghetto. Could you elaborate on this?

SINGER: The special character of Yiddish is not only in the language, it's also in the character of those who speak Yiddish, the *Weltanschauung* of the Yiddish-speaking people. Those who spoke Yiddish for hundreds of years were different from the Jews who spoke French or English and now speak Hebrew. What I mean is, the Yiddish-speaking man is an outsider to the world because his parents and grandparents for generations back have lived in ghettos. There is one thing which they all have in common and this is a feeling that this world and its good things, and all its hopes, are not really of any tremendous importance. The men of the ghetto understood many things which the men outside the ghetto did not. For example, if you insulted a squire or a lord or a baron by saying that his wife has a hooked nose, he would immediately call for a duel, and it was his death or your death. He could not take any insult, while the man in the ghetto never had any such thing as a duel. When one man insulted another, the insulted one would say, "He's a coarse man," or "He's a sinner who will go to Gehenna in the next world." But he would not endanger his or the other's life.

There wasn't this kind of pride which the people had when they were French or Russian or English. The Yiddish-speaking man was not a man of worldly pride. There was no place in the ghetto for being proud, for fighting over a beautiful lady or admiring the ladies the way the knights did. There was a kind of built-in passivity in these people, a feeling that everything is vanity and the best a man can do is just wait and see what destiny can bring.

BURGIN: I'm curious about when you were last in Israel.

SINGER: In 1975, when they gave me an honorary doctorate.

BURGIN: Do you have any ambivalent feelings about the country?

SINGER: No, no. I love Israel. I feel that for two thousand years the Jew was in exile and our enemies always said to us, "Go back to Israel." They always said to us, to the Jew, "What are you doing here in Europe?" So finally, after two thousand years of suffering, some of our young people felt, if the world does not belong to us, if we are strangers in Europe, if we are strangers everywhere, let's have a country of our own. Now they tell them, "Go back to Poland, go back to Russia." So where should the Jew go? Since people kept on driving us back to the land of our ancestors, we went back there, and I hope to God that the children of Ishmael will not always fight with the children of Isaac, but will make peace, and that there will be a place for the Jewish state.

BURGIN: Your son lives there, and your grandchildren live there?

SINGER: I have four grandchildren and they were born there.

BURGIN: Do you speak with them in Yiddish? In Hebrew?

SINGER: If I speak to them, it's in halting Hebrew.

BURGIN: Have you had much contact with Yiddish-speaking Jews in New York?

SINGER: Well, if I have any contact with Jews, it's mostly with Yiddish-speaking Jews, of course. Now that I've learned English I am also in contact with English-speaking Jews. All my life I lived among them. When I was young, I felt, why are they so humble, and why are they so pessimistic, and why do they keep on thanking the Almighty for every trouble they have? But I admire their humility just the same.

BURGIN: I think you said once that you didn't really associate with the Yiddish-speaking Jews, let's say in Brooklyn, because you felt that something was missing.

SINGER: The Yiddish-speaking Jew is a little different here, because he doesn't have to be so humble as in Poland, Russia, or Rumania. Here he's an American citizen, he gets an American passport. When he goes to France, he's an American and treated like one. But just the same, they are basically the same as they were in Poland.

BURGIN: When you're alone with your wife, do you speak English or Hebrew?

SINGER: We speak English. She was born in Germany.

BURGIN: Perhaps the fact that you never had many deep personal relationships with Yiddish-speaking people in this country served as a catalyst to base so much of your fiction on those Jews whom you knew before you came here. You lived more in memory than in the present?

SINGER: As long as I have to write about Yiddish-speaking people, I would rather write about those who spoke Yiddish in Poland.

BURGIN: They are more real to you, more vivid?

SINGER: I knew their way of thinking better. Even if I write about America, I still write about Yiddish-speaking people. I almost never write about people born in this country. The heroes of my stories and novels, even if they speak English, are immigrants who came here and barely learned the language.

BURGIN: Let me ask you a bit about your plays. *Yentl the Yeshiva Boy* and *Teibele and Her Demon* are your two best-known plays. What part did you play in adapting them from your short stories?

SINGER: I adapted Teible together with a Miss Eve Friedman. She gave me advice, she encouraged me, and so on, but actually I did all the writing myself. *Teibele* follows the original story, but we enlarged it to make it into a play. I saw it in Minneapolis . . .

BURGIN: Were you satisfied with the way it was produced?

SINGER: The ending didn't come out the way I wanted. There was something wrong with the ending.

BURGIN: Is there anything you want to say about the big reaction to your *Yentl* self-interview about the Barbra Streisand film in the New York *Times?*

SINGER: No, I did not like the movie and I said so. How can a person born in this country really describe a Yeshiva the way it is? When a writer or director or anybody else tries to give a milieu which is not his, he will make millions of mistakes—little mistakes, but they're mistakes. Of course, a great writer like Shakespeare did not care, because he was a poet, his ambition was in language and in expressing general ideas and also in creating tension. He was not a realist. But I am a realist. Even when I write about demons, they are not just general demons, they are demons of particular towns and they speak the language of the people. So for me, when I see a Yeshiva and the Yeshiva boys are dressed differently, speak differently than they really did, I feel that the whole thing does not really give us anything. If the individuality is lacking, everything is lacking.

BURGIN: I know you are very fond of Chekhov's stories. Do you have an equal admiration for his plays?

SINGER: He is my favorite writer of short stories, but a play where people sit and express moods is not really theater.

BURGIN: Then you don't particularly like Chekhov as a playwright?

SINGER: I love his stories . . .

BURGIN: But not his plays?

SINGER: I never saw enough really to have an opinion.
You know that Tolstoy once said to Chekhov, "Do me a
favor and don't write plays." I think that a play must
have action, but Chekhov was so good that even if he
gave you a play that was all mood, I'm sure it would
contain little treasures.

BURGIN: Since we are talking about your writing in
forms outside of fiction, I'd like to ask you about your
memoirs. You began them late in life and the four
volumes that you've published bring you only as far as
your thirties. Do you plan to continue?

SINGER: All my writing is actually a memoir—a writer
gets all of his material from his life. From the people he
meets. So even if I write about other people it is a part
of my memoirs. Because of this I am planning to continue my memoirs one way or another.

I don't see any basic difference between my fiction
and my memoirs. I think it's true not only in my case
but for all writers. When you read the classic writers
you find in every work they did parts of their lives.
When you read *Satan in Goray*, my first book, you will
find there parts of my life. For example, Rabbi Benish,
whom I describe there, is actually my maternal grandfather.

BURGIN: How do you feel about writing non-fiction,
and about writing with yourself as the central character?

SINGER: In all my books I am there—my character is there in one way or another. I haven't yet found a serious writer who doesn't write about himself and his life. You recognize Tolstoy in *War and Peace*. He is called Pierre. And in *Anna Karenina* he is called Levin. But it is always Tolstoy.

BURGIN: What kinds of things are you working on now? Plays, novels, children's books, stories?

SINGER: At this time, I am writing a novel which is called *The Way Home*. It is again the story of a penitent, only enlarged, and I hope also enriched. *The Penitent* concentrated on his penance, but I wrote little about the protagonist's sins. In this book I concentrate on both his sinful life and the way he left it behind.

This season I hope to have three plays performed: *Teibele and Her Demon* in the Habimah (in Israel); *Shlemiel the First* will be produced in English translation in New York and a play in Yiddish in Montreal. Although I never consider myself a playwright, plays come from my pen one way or another—almost against my will.

BURGIN: If I might change the subject—I can't help remembering once when we were talking over the phone and you were so happy about a story that was coming out in *The New Yorker*. I thought: Here is this man who's always said, "Writers can't change the world, we can't even make it worse" and "Writers are only entertainers" and "I don't see God's mercy" and "The world is a jungle and a slaughterhouse," and this same person is so happy about a story being published. What gives you joy in writing?

SINGER: It is like the exiled Jew who, when he lives through a day, feels, thank God, I lived this day, no great misfortune happened. I feel the same thing about writing. I know that the dangers in writing are great. You may have a lot of talent, but still you can write a very bad novel and a very bad story. For me, if I reread my story and I see that it's not bad, I consider it a miracle. I don't take it for granted that I will sit down and write a good story, because by nature you don't write a good story. It never comes out right from the beginning. You have to work on it. In literature, as in love and sex, there are no guarantees.

BURGIN: But in light of your world view, what accounts for that joy in writing? Why rejoice in something that you see as such a minor activity?

SINGER: No matter how pessimistic a human being is, just the same, if something good happens to him he will be joyful.

BURGIN: Isn't that strange?

SINGER: This is human nature. They say that when Schopenhauer read a chapter of his work *The World as Will and Idea* and it came out well, he became very happy. When an undertaker has a good day he comes home and he's beaming with joy.

BURGIN: So we really don't know the answer.

SINGER: God has given us a kind of selfishness, because if not, we would destroy ourselves. If man would not love himself, he would knock his head on the rocks. He would fight with every man. He would get into millions of dangers, even more than he does today. Even though I feel that literature cannot save the world, if I manage to write a story which I think is right, and if I see that the printer did not make a million mistakes, which in Yiddish happens almost all the time, I am grateful. This doesn't mean that I've lost my pessimism. I still know that human life is a misery, and I still know that literature will not save the world, and I still know that other things will not save it either, but, just the same, I feel that whatever a human being does he should try his best, and I don't blame him if it gives him a little temporary satisfaction. Because a pessimist expects little, he is able to appreciate the little gifts God is bestowing on us.

BURGIN: As far as the happiness of your readers of *Shosha* is concerned, some of your critics were a bit taken aback by your so-called abrupt ending. Personally, I thought it was among the most beautiful and artistically daring passages in the book. Would you say that one of the reasons you left out, or didn't dramatize in detail, what happened to some of the characters is that you'd already done this before in *The Family Moskat?*

SINGER: Some of the readers would have liked this book to be like *The Family Moskat.* Of course, if it would have been like *The Family Moskat,* they would have said he repeats himself. I wanted to write it differently, in a different style, shorter, avoid anything which is not essential to the story. And in a way it is my personal experiment.

BURGIN: Is that why in the epilogue the narrator speaks in such a deadpan way, just one sentence or one line to describe the death of his former friend?

SINGER: By the way, although it is written in the first person, my part in this novel is very small. I try to make other things bigger.

BURGIN: It's the situation, the milieu that really dominates.

SINGER: And the unexplained passion of this half-retarded person. The whole thing is kind of subdued. It's not the story of a highly passionate love that you might see in *The Family Moskat* between Hadassah and Asa Heshel, or between Jacob and Wanda in *The Slave*. The passion here is subdued because the protagonist knows that it takes place in an atmosphere of death.

13.

The Penitent . . . Vegetarianism . . .
Misplacing things . . . *Hunger* . . . Modern
unhappiness . . . My work is my drug . . .
Everyday life

BURGIN: I'd like to ask you some questions about your
recently translated novel, *The Penitent*. I'm sure many
readers are curious to know how fully you endorse
Shapiro's criticism of modern culture. For example, he
expresses a great disdain for modern literature and psy-
chiatry.

SINGER: Actually, he expresses disdain for all literature, not only modern. By literature I mean worldly
literature. From his point of view, stories of love, of sex,
or of human cruelty and war don't do anything for the
reader. They give him an appetite either for sex or for
fighting. From Joseph's Jewish point of view, this is a
waste of time, and a waste of time is actually a sin,
because at the same time one could be studying the
Torah or fulfilling some of God's commandments. The
point of view that literature is nothing, that literature is
really an implement of Satan, is very old. They used to
call it *sforim chitzonim*, which means "outside books,"
or books which have nothing to do with Jewish religion,
not kosher. Of course, I cannot say that I share this

view. If I shared it, I would behave like Shapiro and would not keep writing. I wouldn't publish anything.

BURGIN: But don't some of the things he says express certain of your feelings?

SINGER: In some cases, yes. Since I was born in a home where my parents thought like Joseph Shapiro, I know exactly how he thinks. Still, the tendency to identify a protagonist with a writer is a very silly one. Some people came to the conclusion that Dostoyevsky really was a murderer. Give him freedom and he would kill a Russian woman and her niece and so on. It's ridiculous. The fact that you know the way of thinking of a murderer does not mean that you are a murderer. It means that you can project yourself into his way of thinking. This is the very essence of talent. But this suspicion that the writer is always the hero of his book can do great damage to literature. Joseph Shapiro represents himself. He represents the extreme Orthodox Jew for whom the Torah is everything, and everything beside the Torah is nothing. To say that I preach it myself is really a way of trying to sabotage literature.

BURGIN: Let me ask you something else that I know you have strong feelings about. I recently reread "The Slaughterer," which is a very powerful indictment of the casual slaughter of animals. You also emphasize this in *The Penitent.* I was wondering about your vegetarianism.

SINGER: In this case no one can suspect that I am really a slaughterer. I really feel that sensitive people, people who think about things, must come to the conclusion that you cannot be gentle while you're killing a creature, you cannot be for justice while you take a creature which is weaker than you and slaughter it, and torture it. I've had this feeling since I was a child and many children have it. But somehow my parents told me that this means that I am trying to have more compassion than the Almighty. My mother told me that if I become a vegetarian I will die from hunger, from malnutrition. So I was afraid, I said, "Well, what can I do?" But at another stage of my life, about twenty years ago, I felt that I would be a real hypocrite if I would write or speak against bloodshed while I would be shedding blood myself. There's nothing profound about it, it's just an emotion. It is the way I feel. It is just common sense to me that if you believe in compassion and in justice you cannot treat the animals the very opposite simply because they are weaker or because they have less intelligence. It's not our business to judge these things. They have the type of intelligence they need to exist.

BURGIN: How did your older brother feel about this?

SINGER: My brother also felt the same way.

BURGIN: Was he also a vegetarian?

SINGER: He did eat meat. Many feel the way I do, but just the same they say, "What will I accomplish by this? The animals will be eaten anyhow, and if they are not eaten by people, they will eat one another.

BURGIN: How can you be certain that vegetables don't have souls, too? They grow, they live.

SINGER: You cannot be sure, but you cannot go so far. This would mean that every person who is a vegetarian should actually commit suicide, which is also not right. We have no proof that vegetables suffer, we have not yet heard of a potato running away from the pot.

BURGIN: Some people believe they can converse with plants.

SINGER: They like to believe so to prove that vegetarianism is nonsense.

BURGIN: Another story of yours I reread recently was "The Lecturer" and I noticed in that story that once again you use the theme of someone losing something. That recurs in a number of your stories.

SINGER: From my childhood I used to misplace things —I didn't pay attention to where I put them. In a way I feel that all people are losers in a big way. This theme is also connected with old age, since people keep on losing things more and more as they get older.

BURGIN: Eventually they lose their time.

SINGER: Yes. I know many people, old people, tell me they are always searching for things, because they don't remember where they put them. Since I often describe older people and I also describe young people who behave like old people, this theme occurs all the time to me. There's not a day when I don't lose a manuscript, or think that I lost it, and keep on searching for it. Now my wife, who is a few years younger than me, is also searching all the time for things. Also, society's development increases our chance of losing things, because in olden times people didn't have large apartments, they didn't have so much furniture, they didn't have so many things. Letters didn't come all the time. So they did not have a chance to misplace things the way we do today. Also, people did not travel all the time. Today I just came back from San Francisco and Los Angeles, and I might have lost on the way some of my speeches and manuscripts.

BURGIN: So you're emphasizing our sense of confusion in the world. How fragile our sense of security and belonging is.

SINGER: Yes, it is a weakness. And it is also a result of the many things people are doing in our time, which they are doing more and more and more.

BURGIN: In reading over some of our earlier conversations, I was somewhat surprised, since so much of your own writing deals with your memory of your past, that you don't have more enthusiasm for Proust.

SINGER: It was difficult for me to read *Remembrance of Things Past* because I couldn't read it in French, and years ago it was hard for me to read the translation in English. Also, Proust writes directly about the emotions —while I don't.

BURGIN: You dramatize more.

SINGER: I describe the things or events which create emotion. I won't ever say about a man "he felt badly"; instead I'll say he has a bellyache or a headache, or he was losing things. I describe things from which you learn whether he is happy or unhappy. As I've said before, words which express emotions are few in number and have become so banal that they have lost their meaning. Because of this I didn't like reading Proust too much, because he used these direct words—"he was happy, he was unhappy, he was disturbed." He still used these words because in his time they hadn't been so misused. Today they are misused by psychologists and by journalists. I hate analysis in literature, and Proust, although he was a good storyteller, was also a big analyzer.

BURGIN: When you use demons in your fiction, is that one way you represent emotions without analyzing them? How did demons become a regular feature of your writing?

SINGER: They always were ever since I began to write. Stories about demons are folklore, really, and folklore tells stories, it doesn't analyze emotions.

BURGIN: In "Geitzel the Monkey" you say, "What are demons if not imitators?" I wonder if you can comment on what you meant by that.

SINGER: These words ("The demon is an imitator") themselves are folklore, because the feeling of a child who looks into a mirror is that of a primitive man who's surprised by an imitator. You put out your tongue, he will do the same thing. You scratch your nose, the image in the mirror will do the same thing. By the way, I was taught in my own house that the mirror is full of demons.

156

BURGIN: I know you have fondness for Knut Hamsun's book *Hunger.*

SINGER: Yes, I wrote an introduction to it.

BURGIN: Did that book influence your aesthetics?

SINGER: I read it as a child.

BURGIN: What appealed to you?

SINGER: *Hunger* didn't appeal to me as much as his novel called *Pan,* which is a masterpiece. Hamsun was not an analyzer at all. I would say what was great about Hamsun is that he described love as a kind of fight. Lovers sometimes are inclined to fight—it is a struggle between two people—and sometimes there's a lot of malice in it, a lot of vengeance, and the strong one tries to make the other weak, even weaker than he or she is. Hamsun had a great feeling about the spite which goes together with love. He could describe it better than any other writer. In *Pan* these two people, Edward and Edwarda (the name of the girl), keep on fighting one another. They are actually waging a war. The war of love was Hamsun's topic.

BURGIN: The novelists you express the most admiration for are invariably nineteenth-century writers. I know you're disenchanted with the direction of much of twentieth-century literature. Can you explain further why you feel this way?

SINGER: I would say the only trouble with the second half of the twentieth century is that it doesn't contain enough stories, and because the writers don't have a story to tell, their words become clichés and meaningless.

BURGIN: Why has this happened to literature now?

SINGER: Because modern man has become more and more interested in abstractions and rules. His mind works in a scientific way. He just refuses to go into the life of a single, unique person. If he writes a love story he wants it to express many love stories. It has to be the love story of all love stories. He's not satisfied with saying, "Here is a unique love story which happened in a unique place in a special time which has never happened before and will never repeat itself," because then it loses all scientific value and all sociological value. It loses all value from his point of view.

The writer of the nineteenth century, however, was very happy to say, "Here is something which happened once, it could only happen in Russia in such and such a place, it might never happen again." The scientific mind runs away from the unique; the unique mind runs away from psychology and from rules.

BURGIN: Do you also feel that a lot of contemporary writing suffers from a surfeit of introspection, even solipsism?

SINGER: If you say about a man "he was unhappy," the word "unhappy" means nothing. We don't know why he's unhappy. You can be unhappy because you have no sex or because you didn't get a Ph.D. The words that express emotions must always be explained by deeds. Today many of these words have become such clichés that no writer really uses them. You will never see Chekhov say "this man was unhappy" or "this man was happy." Instead he gives the reader some facts or deeds which will explain his characters' emotions. The emotions must be connected with a story. Without a story they don't express anything.

BURGIN: I know you have some serious misgivings about modern society, apart from its literary values. Can you describe this spiritual crisis in a general way? Why, for example, are so many people increasingly turning to alcohol or drugs?

SINGER: I would say that modern man and especially young men are unhappy because of a lack of religion, and I don't mean the organized religions so much as the belief in higher powers. For many thousands of years people believed in God or they believed in gods. They believed that the world is not just an accident and that the powers which rule the world judge the world and pay back good with good and bad with bad. Of course, the pagans did not believe the way, let's say, the Jews believed, but even so there was a belief in higher powers and in justice. They believed that there are men to whom God reveals Himself who really know what they are doing. Even the little belief which people had in humanism was destroyed by so many terrible wars and revolutions and by such people as Stalin and Hitler. Those people also considered themselves humanists, by the way, since they spoke in the name of humanity, and even called themselves socialists.

Because of all this, modern man feels as if he's playing in a lottery. Either he will succeed or he will fail, but he doesn't believe there's any real power which takes care of things. There is now a great kind of disappointment in people. I would say that never in human history have so many people been disappointed in everything and had so much doubt about everything than today. Of course, in Soviet Russia they force them to say that they believe, but they don't believe and they know that they are being led like sheep. This is the reason for the widespread use of drugs. Even if the police saw to it that the drug dealers were arrested or destroyed, the need for drugs would still be there.

BURGIN: What can ever turn things around or are things going to get even worse?

SINGER: I don't think that the despair will reach a degree where the whole of humanity will commit suicide. Men are now so often disappointed in marriage. For thousands of years somehow man believed that when he left his home, he left near the fire a faithful wife. This belief is disappearing; literature, the movies, the plays in the theater, they all make mincemeat out of the institution of marriage. They show, rightly so, that faithfulness is disappearing.

BURGIN: If someone is faithful for a year now it's a major accomplishment.

SINGER: So modern man feels that he has really nothing to live for. He has nothing really to work for, and with such a mood, people cannot last long. I think that in the Communist countries they give them a kind of surrogate of a belief. They make them say that Lenin was the leader and he knew everything. But in the capitalistic countries there isn't even such a would-be leader. So because of all this I think that men are more disappointed and more unhappy than they ever were. Also, modern man does not really believe in free will at all. His whole culture is geared to deny it. Everything is explained as a result of either evolution or revolution. Actually, I wouldn't say that a man can do everything he wants to, but he can always make a choice. If he cannot make a choice in one way, he can make a choice in another way. He is a free agent. But modern science, psychology, biology, philosophy, the whole modern way of teaching people is that man is a product. For instance, when you interview me you often ask me, "Why did you do this?" The reason you ask me those questions is that we are all so accustomed to thinking that everything we do is a *result* of something, that if I would tell you, "I do it because I *want* to do it," it would seem to you anti-scientific. What do you mean, you *want* to do it? You are *compelled* to do it. The only thing is, you have to discover *why* you are compelled. This is how many people think today.

BURGIN: I guess in a way the taking of drugs is another abdication of free will.

SINGER: It is as if a man would say, "Since I have no free will anyhow, why not take something that can draw me out of it, give me some good dreams or fantasies?" Because taking drugs is a way of dreaming while being awake.

BURGIN: Of shutting out the world and creating a new universe.

SINGER: For a short time.

BURGIN: We talked before about your difficult early days in America when you felt so alien. In fact, you called one of your recent memoirs *Lost in America*. Do you still feel alien in this country, and if so, in what way?

SINGER: I don't feel lost in America, I feel lost in the world. I feel just like all those people I described. I don't take drugs because my work is my drug. I try to forget myself in my work, but I have the same doubts and the same terrible feelings as all the others who do take drugs. I grew up in a house which was full of faith, and over the years my faith diminished. Today, I still believe in God. I still don't believe that the world was a physical or a chemical accident and that some cosmic *bomb* exploded and created the universe. I still believe that there was a plan and that there was more to it than some silly accident that happened twenty billion years ago (which the "scholars" speak about as if it happened yesterday, they are so *sure* that it happened). I cling in a way to this belief that there are higher powers, that there is a God. I can believe in God's wisdom but I cannot see His mercy. His mercy or His providence is more hidden in our times than ever.

BURGIN: Let me ask you about one other issue of our time. You've spoken out or written about many atrocities, but to my knowledge you've never specifically written or commented about nuclear arms or the possibility of a global holocaust. I wonder what your thoughts are about that, or whether you think it can be written about in fiction.

SINGER: No. I think that language is really too limited to write about it.

BURGIN: What about the potential great cruelty of the nuclear holocaust?

SINGER: The potential is not fiction. I don't write about "potential."

BURGIN: Why not?

SINGER: I'm not a sociologist. Literature is about the past, not about the future.

BURGIN: But we *are* living in a world where all life could now become extinct, very easily.

SINGER: Yes, this is true, but you cannot write a story about an atomic bomb which would fall in the future. I can as a human being say that the atomic bomb may kill millions of people, but everybody can say this. Anybody, a child of six years can say this. In this respect, I cannot be more effective or clearer than this child.

BURGIN: Let me ask you about your everyday life for a moment. What are your days like in Miami? Are they planned, improvised, or half and half?

SINGER: They're not completely improvised. In the morning I go down to the drugstore to have breakfast as I've done for years since I've come here. And then I take walks. Every day I walk at least five miles.

BURGIN: On the beach, or in any particular direction?

SINGER: No, I walk in the shopping center. If the weather is bad I even walk in the corridor. I open the window there and I get some air . . . I see to it that I walk every day. If not, I would become physically stagnant.

BURGIN: Do you think while you walk or do you walk to relieve yourself from thinking?

SINGER: Sometimes I get ideas, sometimes I just think any thoughts or fantasies or whatever occurs to my mind.

BURGIN: Besides your wife, who are the people who you're closest to?

SINGER: Wherever I am—in New York or Miami or Switzerland—my closest friends are the people I work with: my publishers, editors, translators, my secretary, all the people who teach and publish and enhance my work. Many people visit me, many call me and invite me to lecture or to attend receptions . . .

Of course, I am close to my family . . . maybe not as close to them as I should be. My translators, of course, play a big part in my life, and so do my editors. But I'm not really a family man. I don't think about them all the time . . .

I didn't marry until I was thirty-five years old. For years I was against marriage altogether. I was in a way influenced by the famous Jewish German writer Otto Weininger, who considered women and the institution of marriage a major disturbance to men of spirit. But all these decisions which young people make are bound to be broken by life. At a certain time of my life I felt that without a home I would not be able to continue my literary career. At that time I met my present wife,

Alma, and I felt that here was the person whom destiny sent to me. We have been married over forty years now and I never regretted it. Let me quote here a writer who was asked if he ever thought about divorce and whose answer was: "About killing her, many times— but never about divorcing her." There are a number of conflicts between husband and wife which can never really be solved, but where there is love the bad things are quickly forgotten and the good things are remembered.

BURGIN: Who are your other personal friends?

SINGER: I still have some friends from the olden times. I'm not completely lonesome, neither am I much of a mixer.

BURGIN: Is that the way it's been most of your life in Florida?

SINGER: In the summer I go to Switzerland.

BURGIN: Each summer?

SINGER: Yes, each summer. I spoke in Zurich one fall for a huge crowd of people. Many people could not get into the theater. I spoke in English, in German, and in Yiddish. Swiss people who speak German understand Yiddish better than many others.

BURGIN: May I ask you what interests you have or have had in the other arts, in painting or music?

SINGER: I didn't have any education in music, I don't know what it is. Of course, I like classical music better than jazz, but that's all I can say.

BURGIN: It's never been important in your life?

SINGER: I sometimes sing songs which they sang in Poland in Warsaw. But music is not my world. About painting I have a notion, but I completely dislike this abstract, symbolic painting where they make a few smudges and say, "This means this, this means that." I don't give a hoot what they mean. They don't interest me at all. And the theater, I do like, but I seldom go. It's difficult to go to the theater. I can live without it. I would say that, for me, literature is *the* art.

BURGIN: You wrote poems at one point in your life, didn't you?

SINGER: Not really, I only wrote a few things when I needed to incorporate them into my fiction.

BURGIN: I meant when you started writing.

SINGER: I tried in Hebrew, but I knew almost immediately that I have to be a prose writer, not a poet.

BURGIN: Do you think that having an older brother who was a successful writer inhibited your development as a writer in any way?

SINGER: No. The opposite is true.

BURGIN: A number of your critics or biographers have suggested it.

SINGER: They like to say so, but actually he was my teacher of literature. I learned a lot from him, and his death caused me great anguish which has never healed. Sometimes we quarreled as brothers do, we quarreled once in a while, but the idea that I went around and felt that he was in my way and didn't let me grow is as false as can be. The very opposite is true. He made me grow.

BURGIN: How did you develop your own voice as a writer?

SINGER: It developed when I discovered that I should write about my environment, which means the Jewish people, the Yiddish-speaking people. I never try to write just about "people" or humanity in general. I learned that the literary masters all wrote about specific kinds of people, like Flaubert, who wrote about the French, and Gogol, who wrote about the Ukrainian people, and so on. I made up my mind that the Yiddish-speaking people, whether they lived in America or in Poland, are the people whom I know best. I know best their language and their way of thinking. And I stay with this. Through my stories I say whatever I can say. Sometimes the story has no message whatsoever and this doesn't bother me at all. I don't have to keep on pouring out messages. I think I told you that the Ten Commandments are such a good message that we don't need any more. The only thing we need is to learn how to keep them.

14.

The hedonist and the Rabbi . . . Suicide is
often heroic . . . The wolf and the sheep
. . . A few lines

BURGIN: In *The Estate* you describe two death scenes:
Clara's death, where she has the experience of leaving
her body, and Rabbi Jochanan's death. These two people, in the way they conduct their lives, couldn't have
been further apart. I take it this wasn't a coincidence.
Was there an attempt to make a kind of parallel or
contrast with the two scenes, having them intentionally
juxtaposed in the ways they experience death?

SINGER: Just as the lives of these two people were not
alike, so their deaths were not alike. They couldn't have
been alike because Clara was a hedonist. She wanted to
get all the pleasure of life and she did not succeed. Just
the same, when I describe her death I describe it so that
the feeling is that she's not lost forever. She's not extin-
guished. I make the reader feel that even with Clara,
although she was a sinner and a person who betrayed
people and lied and was selfish to a high degree, just the
same there is dignity even in her dying. She is not gone
forever. There must be some place where Clara's soul is
going, either to be cleansed or whatever they do with
souls. On the other hand, Rabbi Jochanan was a saint

and he dies like a saint. I make him see a light which no human eye, no healthy human being, has ever seen. Whether I try to make this as a parallel, I'm not sure, because I wrote about Jochanan's death many months after I wrote about Clara's death, and to make parallels consciously is not really in my nature. In both cases I speak more or less about immortality, but the immortality of a saint and the immortality of a selfish and reckless person are not the same. They have different qualities altogether.

BURGIN: That's a little bit ambiguous. What do you mean by different qualities?

SINGER: I mean the experience of dying is different for both of them. Clara doesn't have that blissful feeling of unity with God.

BURGIN: Are you hinting that there's an eternal life for both of them?

SINGER: If the reader assumes that what I tell is true, that she really went out of the body and the Rabbi saw such a light, then of course this means that both go into another world. However, if the reader is not a believer, he could say it was completely subjective. They both had hallucinations, imagined it.

BURGIN: And what did you intend?

SINGER: Well, I would say that when I write about such things, I always make them ambiguous, because since I myself am not sure how things are, why should I try to make the reader sure.

BURGIN: How would you describe your belief?

SINGER: I believe in some kind of life after death, but since there is no evidence of it, I don't want to come out to the people and say it is so. I make it so that the believer will say here is immortality, while the non-believer will say it's simply the writer's *belief* in immortality. I've done this in almost all my stories about the supernatural. They can always be explained in either a subjective or an objective way.

BURGIN: Still, you close the "Clara" section with the line "She's a fragment of eternity."

SINGER: Of course, about this there is no question whatsoever. We are all fragments of eternity.

BURGIN: In what sense?

SINGER: We are a part of the universe and the universe is certainly eternal. Even if you don't believe in miracles, we are still a fragment of eternity.

BURGIN: In *The Family Moskat* you end with the line "Death is the Messiah. That's the real truth." Do you still feel that way, twenty-five years later?

SINGER: I still feel that way, that on this planet death is the only sure redemption. Because all the other redemptions disappoint us, they are promises that are never kept. But the promise which death gives to people is always kept.

BURGIN: This isn't easy to ask you, but do you think more about death now than when you were younger?

SINGER: No. I was thinking about death when I was eighteen, seventeen, and most probably twelve and thirteen years old. The problem of death was always before me because I saw people dying in our street. The funeral wagons were always there. People who a day before yesterday came to the prayer house to pray, two days later were already taken to the cemetery. I saw all this and I was puzzled, frightened, astonished.

BURGIN: You still think about it?

SINGER: I still think about it.

BURGIN: Do you try to push it out of your mind?

SINGER: No. I don't push it out of my mind.

BURGIN: What are your thoughts?

SINGER: Since there is no scientific proof that there is immortality, that the soul lives, it's all a question of belief. I know as much about it today as I knew when I was twelve years old. I say to myself, "What is the sense of all this living and all this effort and hoping when by the attack of some microbe everything a human being has experienced and has gathered together is finished?"
All people think about death. The only thing is, some people don't have the time, they cannot afford to think much about it. These people have such a passion for life that they think about it until their very last day . . . I heard of a man who was very much interested in the

stock market. On the last day of his life the stocks went up and he was kind of happy, in fact he died smiling. When a man has such a passion for earthly things, he just doesn't have the time to think about death, or it may be this passion for earthly things is a way of pushing away his thoughts about death. Why think about death if you can think about the stocks? Maybe there is wisdom in it. Spinoza said in his *Ethics* that a wise man never ponders death. He thinks only about life. So from this point of view, the man who was thinking about the stock market till the last hour was a sage. But some people can't push these thoughts away. My feeling is that even the animals have a notion about their death . . .

BURGIN: Only right before the end, though, I think.

SINGER: I've seen them getting old, tired, mellow, resigned to sickness. When a dog gets old he looks at you as if to say: I'm not young anymore, I don't have my old powers. He doesn't think in words, but his eyes express it. You can see it in the eyes of a horse or in some of the other animals.

BURGIN: How would you like to live? What are you trying to accomplish in the rest of your life?

SINGER: I try to do the things which I have been doing for many years—to continue to write because I'm accustomed to it. It is my profession. I always feel that I have some more stories to tell. I would also like once to write a book that would sum up my thoughts or feelings about life, a non-fiction book. Whether I will succeed in doing it, I don't know, because I've never really written such books, but I toy with the idea of writing a book which would be neither philosophy nor psychology, but a kind of a . . .

BURGIN: Spiritual autobiography. I feel that you've already achieved that in the sum of your work and of course, more specifically, in your memoirs.

SINGER: I once told you that I consider free choice the greatest gift to humanity and I think that people have not really made use of this gift. Sometimes I feel like trying to make good use of free choice, and then if I succeed, to tell people what I did and how I struggled with it.

BURGIN: Since we're discussing death and free choice, I wonder what your feelings are about suicide. Do you believe that suicide is a priori wrong, or are there circumstances that would justify it?

SINGER: No, I think suicide is often heroic.

BURGIN: I'm surprised.

SINGER: Not a man who kills other people and then commits suicide. A person who decides that life isn't worthwhile living and tries to give God's gift back . . . I think that such a person has true courage and shows it by his protest against the evils of life. I think most of the people who commit suicide are people with character and with will power and I admire them. Of course, I would not admire a man who jumped from the fortieth floor when the stocks fell, as happened in 1929, because such a suicide is not a protest . . .

BURGIN: It's not an intellectual decision.

SINGER: It's not a spiritual decision. It's just that yesterday he was worth two million dollars, today he's worth two thousand dollars. He's a sufferer, but there is not much to respect. I think that suicide can be the highest way a man can tell the Almighty, "I don't agree with the way You are managing this world, and because I don't agree, take back Your great gift. I don't want it anymore."

BURGIN: Would you say that suicide is in a certain sense one of the highest ways of the intellect asserting itself over the will, because it's built into us to live, after all?

SINGER: It is as if this person would say, "I've looked over this whole business and I've come to the conclusion that it's of no meaning. My father slept with my mother, and because they wanted this minute of enjoyment, I have to suffer all my life and I don't want it."

It is true that many of the religious people consider suicide a great sin and there is even somewhere a saying—I don't remember if it's in the Talmud or not—that a man who commits suicide loses the world to come. But I've also seen in the Talmud stories of people who did commit suicide, and the Talmud calls them holy people, like Hannah, who lost her seven children and then went up to the roof and threw herself down. It seems that the opinion of the sages about suicide is not unanimous.

BURGIN: Doesn't suicide violate the tenets of almost every religion in the world?

SINGER: Maybe, but I don't care about other people's opinions in this matter. Of course, those who have written religious books held other views. All religions, as far as I can see, are man-made. I don't have to agree with all these men. I never have any special respect for authorities. I don't say that because this man said so I cannot have a different opinion. I would not dare to have a different opinion when it comes to chemistry or physics or medicine, about things which I don't know, but when it comes to such things where no one really knows, I may express my opinion.

BURGIN: Do you think, as Dostoyevsky did, that a good deal of wisdom comes through suffering, or is some suffering purely meaningless?

SINGER: I would say that a wise man gets wiser by suffering. A person without any wisdom may suffer for a hundred years and die a fool. There are no rules to this.

BURGIN: In light of what you just said and in light of the fact that we live in a world where everything survives by living off some other being's death, does this make you feel there's something fiendish about the cosmic scheme of things?

SINGER: I wouldn't say this. I don't have the information. I don't know God, I don't know His thoughts, and I'm sure that if He thinks, His thoughts are infinite times higher than mine. So I cannot judge Him. All I can say is that I can see His wisdom but not His mercy.

BURGIN: How can you reconcile that? How can there be wisdom without mercy?

SINGER: A number of philosophers believed that God is not merciful . . . Spinoza didn't believe that God is merciful. He said He acts according to His laws. I think that Shestov once said there is a God but He's no good. It may be that God is merciful, but since I cannot see it, I would never call Him merciful. I would call Him a God of wisdom, of power. I believe that Malthus expressed ideas which are the very essence of reality. Nothing which was said after Malthus can destroy what he said. I don't have to quote Malthus because I see the same things—that famine and epidemics, deaths and struggle, keep the world in equilibrium. If all the elephants which were produced would live, and all the lions and all the lice, the universe would be full of lice and elephants and lions. Death and suffering are a part of creation, and since I don't like suffering and I don't like to see people and animals struggling against something which is unavoidable, I cannot call God merciful and I feel a great protest in myself against creation. Although there may be an answer, it will never be found on this earth, and since I'm still on this earth, I feel a sense of protest. I think I told you that if I would ever try to create a religion, let's say for myself, I would call it a religion of protest.

I also see that man is merciless, although he himself suffers and dies and is afraid of cancer and heart attacks and all kinds of things. The moment he gets a little power, other people's misfortunes are nothing to him. Since I don't see God's mercy and I see man's cruelty, I'm far from being an optimist.

I once wrote to myself a kind of summing up of what I

see about the world. I wrote it in Yiddish and I can only give you a very short synopsis of it. It begins more or less with a saying like this: Both the wolf and the sheep are dying in misery but no one seems to care about what happens to them. God Himself, the Lord, has created the world so, where the principle of violence and murder is supreme. All I can do in such a world is not really live but smuggle myself through life, sneak by this jungle, hide with my piece of bread before the beasts and murderers catch me.

BURGIN: Can there be a God who isn't merciful and doesn't care about man?

SINGER: I believe that this power is not blind. Even if you don't believe in God, you still believe that there is Nature. The wolf and the sheep are still there and the electrons and magnetic waves are still there, and the atoms and everything else. Whether I say Nature or God, it doesn't make any difference, because I believe that Nature sees. A Nature which sees and thinks is God.

BURGIN: But if Nature sees things without mercy, without pity for man, why should you as a man not revolt against this, why should you support this God?

SINGER: I don't support it . . . I feel the opposite. I say that I'm protesting against this. My relation with God is a relation of protest. I cannot revolt, because to revolt you have to have some power, but to protest you don't need any power. Spinoza said that we have to make peace with Nature, to love God or the Substance intellectually, but I don't say so. I say He's great, He's full of wisdom.

BURGIN: What wisdom, if He causes all this suffering?

SINGER: To create a flower you have to have wisdom. Even though this flower is two hours later eaten up by an ox, we still must admire the wisdom in creating it.

BURGIN: There's wisdom in Mozart and Beethoven, maybe more beautiful than a flower.

SINGER: Oh, no. Far from it. All the professors in the world and all the chemists and all the physicists could not create a flower.

BURGIN: But God's music is not as beautiful as man's. The music of Bach, Mozart, and Beethoven is more beautiful than the wind and the sea.

SINGER: First of all, God created Bach and Beethoven. They are also a part of what God created. So it's all God to the pantheist. To me, God and Nature are the same, except that I believe that Nature is conscious, it knows what it's doing, and if we would know it better we could maybe say it's doing the right thing, but since we don't know and we suffer, we protest. This protest which I express does not maintain that God is bad. I only say He is bad as far as I can see. Because to know what God is I would have to know all the stars and all the planets, the whole universe. You cannot write a review about a book which has a trillion pages after you have read only one. I could say one thing: This page I admire but I don't like it from my point of view. My being a vegetarian is connected with this protest. The man who eats meat or the hunter agrees with the cruelties of Nature, upholds with every bite of meat or fish that might is right. Vegetarianism is my religion, my protest.

BURGIN: For you, then, the universe is like an infinite book.

SINGER: An infinite book of which I've read a few lines. These lines seem to me beautiful but cruel. The best we can do is be silent, but there are times when we must cry out: Why torture the helpless? Why build your glory on our misery? Sometimes I feel that the Almighty is tired of all the praise and the flattery which we pour on Him.

BURGIN: You have been accused at times of being a misanthrope. What kind of misanthropy is it?

SINGER: It consists of not demanding anything from other people, not even from friends—neither money, nor honors, nor recognition. In this epoch where everyone begs—not only the poor but also the mighty, vote for me, buy my merchandise, support my organization, love me, praise me, forgive my crimes—it is a high ideal to abstain from all this beggary. The beggar often carries a knife in his bag. I don't stretch out my hand for any favor. I don't ask for love if it doesn't come by itself.

ISAAC BASHEVIS SINGER received the Nobel Prize for literature in 1978. Born in Radyzmin, Poland, in 1904, he came to the United States in 1935. Mr. Singer's plays, stories, children's books, essays, novels, and memoirs have been translated into numerous languages, including Danish, Hebrew, Swedish, and Norwegian. He and his wife Alma divide their time between New York City and Miami Beach.

RICHARD BURGIN, an assistant professor of English at Drexel University, was founding editor of *New York Arts Journal,* and now edits the literary magazine *Boulevard.* He has published fiction in numerous literary magazines and anthologies. His previous books include *The Man with Missing Parts* and *Conversations with Jorge Luis Borges.*